Jacob's Rod
by
Hilaire Baritel

Translation and additional material
by
Thomas Welton

Foreword by
Michael Sheppard

For more information, please visit www.quareia.com

Foreword copyright 2018 © Michael Sheppard

All rights reserved

Without limiting the rights under copyright reserved above, no part of this publication may be reproduced, stored in, or introduced into a retrieval system, or transmitted, in any form or by any means (electronic, mechanical, photocopying, recording or otherwise) without prior permission of the copyright owner and the publisher of this book.

Published by Quareia Publishing UK

ISBN 978-1-911134-35-0

Foreword

This little book was first printed in 1693, in French, under the title *La Verge de Jacob*. The author was credited as Hilaire Baritel, a publisher of other occult books. This name may, however, be a pseudonym.

In 1875 Thomas Welton, who invented the planchette, translated Baritel's book into English and republished it as *Jacob's Rod*. As well as translating the book he also expanded it somewhat, adding material on trance dowsing and map dowsing. Welton was an interesting character who made his living manufacturing artificial limbs and surgical instruments (as well as planchettes). He was seriously involved with the Spiritualist church, and he was married to a noted crystal gazer and seer.

Regarding the title, "Jacob's rod" is not, in fact, a synonym for "dowsing rod." The name referred originally to a tool called the cross-staff, used in navigation to determine the angle between the horizon and Polaris or the Sun in order to calculate one's latitude. These days, however, the name refers to a ground-penetrating stake used by surveyors as a mount for other instruments.

Jacob's association with this tool has been explained both as a nod to the constellation of Orion, called Jacob on some medieval star charts, and as a reference to chapter thirty-two of *Genesis*, in which Jacob famously wrestles through the night with his angel. We will have more to say about Jacob later in this foreword, but first we should look briefly at the history of the practice of dowsing.

Unlike many forms of divination, whose origins can often be traced back thousands of years, dowsing rods appear to be a fairly recent magical innovation. They are first recorded as in use in 1518, in Germany, when Martin Luther, in his *Decem Praecepta*, declared that dowsing for metals contravened the First Commandment. By 1518 dowsing must therefore have been sufficiently established in Germany for Luther to heartily disapprove of it, but we cannot say for sure how old a practice it already was.

We can, however, say that dowsing's appearance in the historical record probably had to do with its use in Germany's mining industry, which was internationally renowned at the time. Indeed, German miners are known to have spread the technique of dowsing to Elizabeth I's royal mines.

The first mention of using dowsing rods to find water rather than minerals comes slightly later, in a book published in 1573. The book records the life of St. Teresa of Avila, and it describes a friar successfully using a twig to find a water supply for the saint's new convent.

By 1651 the divining rod had added finding buried treasure to its repertoire, as an ancestor of mine, Samuel Sheppard, cynically noted:

> Some Sorcerers do boast they have a Rod,
> Gather'd with Vowes and Sacrifice,
> And (borne about) will strangely nod
> To hidden Treasure where it lies;
> Mankind is (sure) that Rod divine,
> For to the Wealthiest (ever) they incline.

By the end of the seventeenth century, certain dowsing enthusiasts in the South of France were using their rods not only to find hidden metal, water, and treasure, but also to scientifically ferret out criminals and heretics, as a crossed pair of twigs proved a wonderfully unambiguous way to indicate the accused's guilt. Sadly for progressive Western jurisprudence, in 1701 the Inquisition shut down these forward-thinking legalists.[1]

---

[1] Incidentally, the Inquisition is a much-maligned body in the modern occult world. In truth it executed not more than a hundred witches in its whole history, and it was far more concerned with upholding justice than most contemporary secular courts. Records exist of prisoners deliberately committing blasphemy to get their cases transferred to the Inquisition, where they would be assured a relatively fair hearing, and where they would be subjected to no more than *fifteen minutes* of comparatively mild torture, and then only if they couldn't keep their story straight. That the Inquisition

What exactly makes the dowsing rod move has been the subject of intellectual debate since at least 1662, when noted Jesuit scholar Gaspar Schott declared that it was probably Satan doing it. Later, perhaps feeling that he had unfairly blackened the name of the Father of Lies, Schott adopted the more nuanced position that it may or may not be Satan doing it, he wasn't sure.

Schott deserves credit for successfully anticipating, by about a hundred years, the abandonment of Satan as the likeliest agent behind the dowsing rod's movement. Indeed, as the Enlightenment spread across the Western world, the Devil found employment increasingly hard to come by. In the dowsing market he was completely undercut by 'corpuscles,' tiny impersonal *bits of stuff* that, while having none of Old Nick's flamboyance and not yet being any more absolutely provable than he was, came considerably cheaper in terms of belief.

Those who want the details of the corpuscular model of dowsing should refer to William Pryce's 1778 opus, *Mineralogia Cornubiensis.* But briefly, corpuscles could operate much more efficiently than Satan because unlike him they used Science; and though their efficiency came at the cost of a truly personalized service, this had the advantage of very much *not* being a devil's bargain.

---

has a bad reputation today is largely the result of extremely effective past Protestant propaganda, and it testifies to the extent to which history really is written by the victor, England and its colonies being Protestant, and English being today's *lingua franca.*

The other reason that corpuscles came cheaper than Satan was that huddled masses of them already lived in every mineral that might conceivably be dowsed for. They therefore had no need to invoice for the cost of travel to their place of work. On the contrary, yearning to be free, these corpuscles would march eagerly in organized little queues out of the earth at first sight of a dowsing rod, whereupon they were forced to take up residence in its pores due to air pressure—a thoroughly Enlightened and Scientific principle—and due to their desire to *keep the queue moving*—which is a peculiarly English principle, but no less Enlightened for that.

Finally, in 1876, the apparently real explanation for the dowsing rod's movement made its first entrance onto the historical stage, when A. C. Pass and Edward B. Tawney published an article called *The Divining Rod* in Volume I of the Proceedings of the Bristol Naturalists' Society. They presented evidence indicating that dowsers themselves were involuntarily moving their rods in response to unconscious observations they were making of their surroundings, a phenomenon that Pass and Tawney called *cryptesthesia*. The involuntary movements themselves are the result of what is today called the *ideomotor effect*.

What of the possibility that some dowsers, rather than unconsciously responding to their environment, are really responding unconsciously to the instruction of *discarnate beings* who specialize in detecting the presence of underground metal, water, treasure, and heretics?

Well if they are, then the available evidence suggests that these are discarnate beings with a deep distrust of scientific study. (Perhaps they remember what Science did to Satan.) For study after study, including one overseen by celebrated sceptic James Randi, has concluded that dowsers perform no better than chance at locating hidden objects. It should be borne in mind, however, that the same sort of claims have been made regarding the efficacy of homeopathy, and some of the arguments the British Homeopathic Association has made in response[2] apply fairly well to the question of dowsing.

We should also investigate why Martin Luther felt that dowsing contravened the First Commandment, especially if you decide, having read this book, to have a go at it for yourself. (If you are going to imperil your immortal soul, then I want you to be in full possession of the facts.)

The First Commandment reads as follows:

> Thou shalt have no other gods before Me.
>
> — The First Commandment, *Exodus* 20:2 and *Deuteronomy* 5:6.

Admittedly it is not obvious, at first glance, what dowsing has to do with worshipping gods other than

---

[2] https://www.britishhomeopathic.org/evidence/the-evidence-for-homeopathy/

the one of Abraham. Thankfully, the Catechism of the Catholic Church sheds some light on the matter:

> (...) God, however, is the "living God" (Joshua 3:10; Psalm 42:3; etc.) who gives life and intervenes in history.
>
> — Catechism of the Catholic Church 2112

> All forms of divination are to be rejected: recourse to Satan or demons, conjuring up the dead or other practices falsely supposed to "unveil" the future (see for example, Deuteronomy 18:10; Jeremiah 29:8). Consulting horoscopes, astrology, palm reading, interpretation of omens and lots, the phenomena of clairvoyance, and recourse to mediums all conceal a desire for power over time, history, and, in the last analysis, other human beings, as well as a wish to conciliate hidden powers.
>
> — Catechism of the Catholic Church 2116

The reason, then, that dowsing (along with other forms of divination) breaks the First Commandment is that the dowser seeks to manipulate the natural flow of history—something only God has the right to do—by supernatural means. This manipulation is always wrong, whether it involves finding treasure that would otherwise have remained buried, or rooting out ungodly heretics that would otherwise have remained uncombusted.

However, (here's an apple, fancy a bite?) does the assumption made by both Martin Luthor and the Catholic Catechism, that divination is an act that necessarily aims at *subverting* Divine Will, really hold water? For while divination can indeed be used that way, that is far from its best use.

As my parentheses-loving ancestor put it:

> Mankind is (sure) that Rod divine,
> For to the Wealthiest (ever) they incline.

As any mystic worth their salt will tell you, the wealthiest thing to which the divine rod, mankind, may incline is not worldly riches but the knowledge of God. And luckily for us, we actually incline that way naturally, for each of us has a speck of the Divine within us: we are like little magnets who ever want to line up North to South.

But this takes work, for as my dear great great great great great great great great great Uncle Sam pointed out, a *divinely inclining* Rod is

> Gather'd with Vowes and Sacrifice

Our intent to climb Mount God must be as unshakeable as a vow, and we must give up whatever we outgrow as we develop. This is how we polish our magnet. This is how we align ourselves ever better with

God. This is how we make of ourselves a Rod that can truly *divine*, which

> (borne about) will strangely nod
> To hidden Treasure where it lies;

As we develop divinely, the Mysteries begin to reveal themselves. This is the true hidden treasure of divination. (Indeed, the very word 'divination' comes from the Latin *divinare*, "to be inspired by God."

One of the signs of our progression on the Path is the universe starting to speak to us, leaving little messages and hints for us to find as we pass by. We ourselves become divining rods. Equally, divination's best use is as a rod to assist us on our path.[3]

The same holds when you divine for others: the overall aim must be to help set them back on track, to help them move more effectively forwards.

Divination as a tool is best used for "getting right with God"—that is, (re)aligning yourself with your part of the divine plan as it is expressed in the possibilities of your fate path. As a nearly-nameless Egyptian sage put it some four thousand years ago, in the work we today call *The Teachings for King Merykara*:

---

[3] To assist us on our *path*—not to assist us in poking around in the contents of our navels! The Path comes with its own excellent navel lint removal dynamic. Moving forwards is all that is required to activate it.

> Cared for are human beings, the flock of a God who has made heaven and earth for their minds: (...) He has provided magical powers for them as weapons to ward off the arm of happenstance.
>
> — *The Teachings for King Merykara* (from line 131)

Perhaps the same sentiment lies behind the title Hilaire Baritel chose for the book you hold in your hands now, *La Verge de Jacob*, which references a tool named either after the man in the heavens, Orion, or after a chapter from Genesis that is worth quoting here in its entirety:

> 1 And Jacob went on his way, and the angels of God met him.
>
> 2 And when Jacob saw them, he said, This is God's host: and he called the name of that place Mahanaim.
>
> 3 And Jacob sent messengers before him to Esau his brother unto the land of Seir, the country of Edom.
>
> 4 And he commanded them, saying, Thus shall ye speak unto my lord Esau; Thy servant Jacob saith thus, I have sojourned with Laban, and stayed there until now:

5 And I have oxen, and asses, flocks, and menservants, and womenservants: and I have sent to tell my lord, that I may find grace in thy sight.

6 And the messengers returned to Jacob, saying, We came to thy brother Esau, and also he cometh to meet thee, and four hundred men with him.

7 Then Jacob was greatly afraid and distressed: and he divided the people that was with him, and the flocks, and herds, and the camels, into two bands;

8 And said, If Esau come to the one company, and smite it, then the other company which is left shall escape.

9 And Jacob said, O God of my father Abraham, and God of my father Isaac, the Lord which saidst unto me, Return unto thy country, and to thy kindred, and I will deal well with thee:

10 I am not worthy of the least of all the mercies, and of all the truth, which thou hast shewed unto thy servant; for with my staff I passed over this Jordan; and now I am become two bands.

11 Deliver me, I pray thee, from the hand of my brother, from the hand of Esau: for I fear

him, lest he will come and smite me, and the mother with the children.

12 And thou saidst, I will surely do thee good, and make thy seed as the sand of the sea, which cannot be numbered for multitude.

13 And he lodged there that same night; and took of that which came to his hand a present for Esau his brother;

14 Two hundred she goats, and twenty he goats, two hundred ewes, and twenty rams,

15 Thirty milch camels with their colts, forty kine, and ten bulls, twenty she asses, and ten foals.

16 And he delivered them into the hand of his servants, every drove by themselves; and said unto his servants, Pass over before me, and put a space betwixt drove and drove.

17 And he commanded the foremost, saying, When Esau my brother meeteth thee, and asketh thee, saying, Whose art thou? and whither goest thou? and whose are these before thee?

18 Then thou shalt say, They be thy servant Jacob's; it is a present sent unto my lord Esau: and, behold, also he is behind us.

19 And so commanded he the second, and the third, and all that followed the droves, saying, On this manner shall ye speak unto Esau, when ye find him.

20 And say ye moreover, Behold, thy servant Jacob is behind us. For he said, I will appease him with the present that goeth before me, and afterward I will see his face; peradventure he will accept of me.

21 So went the present over before him: and himself lodged that night in the company.

22 And he rose up that night, and took his two wives, and his two womenservants, and his eleven sons, and passed over the ford Jabbok.

23 And he took them, and sent them over the brook, and sent over that he had.

24 And Jacob was left alone; and there wrestled a man with him until the breaking of the day.

25 And when he saw that he prevailed not against him, he touched the hollow of his thigh; and the hollow of Jacob's thigh was out of joint, as he wrestled with him.

26 And he said, Let me go, for the day breaketh. And he said, I will not let thee go, except thou bless me.

27 And he said unto him, What is thy name? And he said, Jacob.

28 And he said, Thy name shall be called no more Jacob, but Israel: for as a prince hast thou power with God and with men, and hast prevailed.

29 And Jacob asked him, and said, Tell me, I pray thee, thy name. And he said, Wherefore is it that thou dost ask after my name? And he blessed him there.

30 And Jacob called the name of the place Peniel: for I have seen God face to face, and my life is preserved.

31 And as he passed over Penuel the sun rose upon him, and he halted upon his thigh.

32 Therefore the children of Israel eat not of the sinew which shrank, which is upon the hollow of the thigh, unto this day: because he touched the hollow of Jacob's thigh in the sinew that shrank.

— Genesis 32, *The Holy Bible (Authorized King James Version)*

Here, Jacob begs God to return to his land and his people and save them from events that promise to spiral out of control as a result of their having strayed from the straight and narrow path. In the chapter which follows,

Esau greets his brother lovingly, and the feared chaos is averted.

Jacob's vision of God face-to-face, wrestling with his angel, was an extreme cure for extreme circumstances. Divination performed in good time allows one to steer the vehicle of one's life in a much gentler manner along the celestial roadways.

And this is worth bearing in mind, whether it is dowsing in particular that you intend to practise, or divination of some other kind. Your work should be necessary, and it should fit into the larger objective of moving forward effectively on the path (yours, someone else's, the land's, etc.). Remember the 'divine' in divination, and remember what really lies behind your wish to find buried treasure... no matter what the treasure that glitters for you may be.

Michael Sheppard, May 2018

JACOB'S ROD:

A TRANSLATION FROM THE FRENCH OF A RARE
AND CURIOUS WORK, A.D. 1693, ON THE
ART OF FINDING SPRINGS, MINES,
AND MINERALS BY MEANS
OF THE HAZEL
ROD.

TO WHICH IS APPENDED RESEARCHES, WITH PROOFS
OF THE EXISTENCE OF A MORE CERTAIN AND
FAR HIGHER FACULTY, WITH CLEAR
AND AMPLE INSTRUCTIONS FOR
USING IT.

PUBLISHED BY THE TRANSLATOR:

THOMAS WELTON,

13, GRAFTON STREET, FITZROY SQUARE, LONDON.

PRICE 2s. 6d.

ALL RIGHTS RESERVED

CONTENTS.

INTRODUCTION	7
CHAPTER I., WHICH SERVES AS AN INTRODUCTION TO THIS TREATISE	9
CHAPTER II., ON THE QUALITY OF THE ROD	12
CHAPTER III., ON THE FORM OF THE ROD	14
CHAPTER IV., ON THE MANNER OF HOLDING JACOB'S ROD, AND HOW IT TURNS	17
CHAPTER V., HOW ONE MAY KNOW IN GENERAL HOW TO DISTINGUISH HIDDEN THINGS BY JACOB'S ROD	21
CHAPTER VI., HOW TO DISCOVER IN PARTICULAR MINES AND HIDDEN METALS	27
CHAPTER VII., BY WHAT MEANS ONE MAY KNOW THE WIDTH OF THE HIDDEN SPRINGS AND MINES	34
CHAPTER VIII., BY WHAT MEANS ONE MAY KNOW THE DEPTH OF SOURCES OR METALS	40
CHAPTER IX., IF ONE CAN TRULY KNOW THE SIZE OF SOURCES OR OF MINES	47
CHAPTER X., OF THE METHOD OF DISCOVERING BOUNDARIES, ROADS, OR PATHS	50
CHAPTER XI., OF THE DIFFERENT CAUSES OF THE ROD'S MOVEMENT	55
CHAPTER XII., EXPLANATION OF SOME DOUBTS UPON THE CAUSES OF THE ROD'S MOVEMENT	65
ADDENDA—CHAPTER I.	78
ADDENDA—CHAPTER II.	99

INTRODUCTION.

In bringing this rare and most curious work before your notice, permit me to say, that from the earliest times it has been observed that all things in nature act powerfully on those persons called by the Baron Von Reichenbach sensitives (especially the metals), causing in them a state of electrical disturbance. This I purpose to teach you how to induce, and by its means find, with almost unerring certainty, mines of metal, minerals, and springs of water, without even the trouble of going to the place where they are situated. At the same time, it is my most earnest request, and I cannot enforce it too strongly, that, should you desire to test my discovery for yourself personally, the strictest attention must be paid to the instructions given, as otherwise inevitably bad results to the sensitive will ensue.

As regards the translation (perhaps it is too literal) allow me to observe that, as far as my experience of twenty-five years goes, some of the explanations and instructions given in it are incorrect (or, at all events, not warranted by actual proofs). However, I will not review the work of M. Baritel in any carping spirit—in the main he is right—but rather put before you in plain language, and I hope clearly, my own experiments with my wife, who has long been privately known to have the precious gift of not only being able to diagnose diseases with exactitude, and so curing the hopelessly sick, but of finding mines, springs, &c., by her faculty, some of which are now in actual work, and producing good results; to them, however, I may not refer, having received remuneration; but much prefer to give ocular demonstration, and, if required, practical instruction.

T. W.

JACOB'S ROD.

A Translation from the French.

CHAPTER I,

WHICH SERVES AS AN INTRODUCTION TO THIS TREATISE.

THE most healthy philosophy allows that the stars influence all sublunary things, and that the quality which is proper and individual to each body, animate or inanimate, depends absolutely, or derives its nature from that which the star impresses on it, which rules over it even from its generation. Experience convinces us every day of this truth, and teaches us at the same time that the knowledge of the chief part of these different qualities are closed letters for men, that certainly they discover some, but there is only the Sovereign Being who has a perfect knowledge of them; and when He permits that mortals draw some of them from the darkness in which their ignorance keeps them buried, it is a benefit which proceeds less from their labour, and from their experience, than from a particular favour which His divine goodness grants to their indigence, and to the relief of their misery, Man, as well as other bodies, and as the most noble participates in these influences; one lives but for war, another for study, and cannot satisfy his curiosity; one seems born for commerce, another to teach, or for agriculture; one loves law and has the spirit of business; the other abhors them, and flies them as contrary to his repose and tranquility; in fine, one is born a poet, another becomes an orator, and, to speak with the apostle Paul to the Ephesians, ch. 4, v. 11, "He gave some apostles," &c., &c.

It is constantly that all these different inclinations of men proceed, and are only impressed on them at the moment of their birth by the different conjunctions or by the different aspects of the planets with the signs, and the other stars which rule or influence.

They are as secondary causes of which God makes use to shed His different gifts upon men, and if by His grace each for himself was happy enough to know the inclination of the star which influences over him principally, he would succeed without difficulty in applying himself to the occupations belonging to it, or would in some degree correct the malignity of it if he were careful to avoid the occasions where it would cause him to sin.

It is not my design to enlarge here upon the proof of this proposition, nor to show how and which are the stars which produce these different effects. Besides this matter being too lofty for me, it would deserve a more ample volume, besides being quite out of my subject. My only object is to treat of those to whom God, by the influence of the stars, has impressed the faculty of discovering, by the movement of the rod called Jacob's rod, all hidden things, subterranean and others.

They maintain that those who have this virtue or faculty are born under the planet Mercury or Saturn, and under the signs of Aquarius and Taurus. We find many who have a similar ascendant, either in all or in part, but I can say there are very few who have a true knowledge of their influence, or who know how to make use of it. It is a hidden treasure, it is a dead power in them, which is entirely useless to them. I will reanimate it in telling them of some experiences which I have or will make on this subject, and, in showing them the use of the rod, I will make them bring into action a virtue which they possessed only as a power. I will also teach those who have not this virtue the means not to be deceived by so many adventurers or others who falsely pretend to have it. In fact every one knows the beauty and the utility of water in a domain—the riches produced by the discovery of mines and of hidden metals; the tranquility and repose given to families by discovering the limits which separate their lands; the place where they ought to be, when by the fraud of the proprietors, or by the succession of the times, they are changed. In a word no one ignores the pleasure of discovering many hidden things about which one is often much troubled, but few people know the way to find them, the place, its depth, its width, the different kinds, the quantity contained, and, in a word, the secret not to make a mistake whilst making the search, and to avoid the great and useless expenses often incurred.

This is what I wish to teach now; the present which I make to the public is as rare as it is new, and I flatter myself that, hitherto, no one has contemplated making a similar one. This thought makes me hope that they will heartily receive a liberality which another doubtless will enrich with a reasoning more solid and better sustained, but not with a more certain experience, and greater frankness than I give it.

I agree that I cannot give it to all equally, because according as the planet or the sign that rules is in the ascendant or descendant (*Appogee, perigee*), or as they concur alone, or joined with other stars of different quality, there are some who have the faculty of discovering generally all sorts of hidden things, others in whom this faculty is very weak, or limited to discover only certain things.

For example, some discover only water, others only mines, others one sort of metal, some only boundaries, in fine, some to whom the rod turns in rising against the stomach, and others to whom it turns in descending to the earth. But, however it may be after making the experiments each will take it after his own way, and all we need observe is that afterwards in speaking of him who holds the rod, one must always understand that the experiments, spoken of ought to be made by one having this *faculty* entire or in part, and that by the terms rod, forked stick, &c., we understand only one and the same thing.

CHAPTER II.

OF THE QUALITY OF THE ROD.

THERE are many who think that the particular talent of a man does not suffice for the discovery of hidden things, that he must have besides a specific instrument formed by nature, or destined for this use. It is why they would choose a certain wood to the exclusion of another, and for this reason they say the green is preferable to the dry, and, amongst the green, that which has the most pith and the most sap has the most effect, for they say its humidity, being of the nature of springs, has more inclination to find its like, hence why they say that the hazel, which has never borne fruit, the white thorn, the wild plum, the willow, and other similar ones, are absolutely necessary for such an operation. But this is an error which can be proved by reason and experience, for the reason, too, that if it were so one must believe that which is not, that the faculty (power) is in the wood alone, that these kinds would produce the same effect to all generally, without distinction of the ascendant, and, in fine, that the kinds of woods growing in the most moist places, or in places containing mines, would be more suited than others to this purpose, because having their roots in the water; by touching with their extremities mines upon which they are grown and have been nourished, they would have been able to retain from them some quality or rapport which would give them a natural inflexion to their centre as to their common country. This error is proved also by experience, which teaches us that all sorts of wood of every kind have an equally rapid and violent movement, and that it is indifferent whether it be green or dry, whether it has been cut by him who uses it or by another, whether it is pithy or not, and though the green wood ought to prevail over the dry, because being full of sap, and the pores more open, transpiration should be more prompt. Nevertheless it seems that if one ought to choose the dry would be preferable to the green, because, wanting moisture, it would be more inclined to search for it, and to bend or turn for that purpose in those places where it is. But as we have said this choice is useless, because they all serve equally, and that if one need make one, it is rather for convenience than necessity; I mean that in use the softest and least rough are more convenient than the others, though they are not of greater effect, whence I draw this conclusion that this virtue or power is not attached to the wood, nor to the instrument one uses, but rather to the efficiency of blood of him who uses it. It is the blood which causes the wood to turn by the impression it communicates to it at the moment the man takes it with his two hands, so that this instrument, whatever its quality, is only a signal of which the man makes use to indicate to him the movement of his blood upon what there is hidden. A mark of this truth is that the dry wood, of whatever nature it may be, turns as easily as the green, and not only the wood, but also iron, silver, brass, wire, whalebone, and other supple and solid matters, excepting in the cases which we will name afterwards.

CHAPTER III.

ON THE FORM OF THE ROD.

HOLY Scripture teaches us that the patriarch Jacob placed some striped rods in the fountains where he watered the cattle of his father-in-law, Laban, so that the impression he had given to them in striping them should communicate itself to the animals whilst drinking, and from them to the little ones to which they would give birth, which has given rise to some to call by the name of Jacob's rod all those they used for the purpose of giving or receiving some impression, and as the forked stick receives a considerable one it has acquired the preceding title; it has also received the name of the Patriarch. There are others who, seduced by the similarity of the effect of this rod with that of Moses, give it the same name, not only because this is susceptible of impression from all kind of matters, as that of Moses was in all the forms he wished to give to it, but also because they say that the miracle that Moses produced in causing water to flow from the rock of Horeb is in some measure reproduced in using this one, by the facility it gives in finding springs in the bosom of the earth or in the hollow of the rocks. But without insisting on these etymologies, which have more of the brilliant than of the solid, since use has fixed it, and that this one serves not only for the discovery of water, but also of all hidden things, we will leave it the name of Jacob's rod, and as that which the Patriarch used was only a stick, such as is generally carried in the hand, many have desired that the one used in the discovery of hidden things should be of that form. It seems that their opinion is not without foundation, not only because it is certain that every kind of rod, as well as every other supple and solid thing which one carries, turns in the hand of him who is born under the planet of which we have spoken, at the moment in which he passes over some spring or mine or hidden thing, but also because in order to ascertain if a person really has this faculty we make him hold his hand open with a stick, similar to the one we have just spoken of, upon the palm of his open hand, and, in the event of its turning or shewing movement in passing over the thing sought for, one concludes that he has this faculty or more, and that the experiment is without fraud, and that is represented in the figure D.

Experience has taught that the simple movement of the rod is not enough to indicate positively the place where the thing is hidden, one has introduced the use of the forked stick made in this form (somewhat like the letter Y) possibly because its movement is more rapid and perceptible, or possibly because in turning in the hand it indicates and marks with the point the place where the hidden thing is, so that it appears as though all the virtue of this indication is enclosed in this point, and that the impression which the stick receives from the two hands which hold it on both sides transfers itself to this extremity in order to shew us what we seek for, from which we draw this certain conclusion, that it is exactly in the place, and opposite to the place where this point lowers itself, that we must dig to find what we seek. I prove this truth not only by natural reason, which teaches us that united forces have more power, and that the impression which the stick receives by its two extremities, communicating and uniting at the end, gives more force to the indication, as being more abundant and vigorous, but also by the experience, inasmuch that if one hides water or metals in two different places, at about a foot's distance from each other, or from that of the extremities of the stick, when the point shall be placed over the one or the other, it will infallibly descend, and if carried into the middle, the two hands being above each to the opposite, it will not descend at all, which clearly justifies the inference we have drawn, that this point serves to mark more justly and certainly the place of the concealed thing. The form of which we have just spoken is also more useful than the simple rod, because one must sometimes dig and search in the clefts of the rocks where mines are, upon the edge of steep places where boundaries may be found, and in other places where space is so limited that the smallness of the place would impede the free movement of the rod, and one would not be able to find the thing sought for, were it not indicated by the end of the forked stick, which being only one foot longer or less can easily be carried everywhere. There is still a reason which inclines us to say that this stick ought to be, it is that if in a same space, or in a small distance, there are many things of different natures hidden. As the stick would give equal movement for all, one would never be able to distinguish of the kinds, as we will presently shew, if the smallness of the stick does not leave us a space to pass from the place of the one to that of the other in order to observe the different causes of its movement.

CHAPTER IV.

OF THE MANNER OF HOLDING JACOB'S ROD AND HOW IT TURNS.

IT is indifferent how one holds the rod, and each person, according to the power of his ascendant, by his prudence and by use, may take a particular posture, as may be most convenient and useful, to make his discovery. However, as those who have not yet practised may be embarassed by ignorance of its use, they will here learn that there are three ways the most usual and frequent to hold it; the first is to hold it straight, the point uppermost, and the backs of the two points closed, against the ground, in this way, marked by the figure A.

The second way is to hold it flat (lying down), the point in front, and the backs of the two points which close it turned against the body, thus, as represented in the figure B.

And the third in a posture which is the middle between these two, by which one holds the point neither entirely up nor entirely in front, but between, as the figure C represents. When one holds it in the first way, in turning it springs up generally against the stomach; when held in the second way in turning it generally descends towards the ground; and when held in the third way it turns indifferently, sometimes on one side, sometimes on the other.

It often does the same in the two first, but from the want of certainty which occurs then, in one and the other, we will draw a certain rule, in order to know the width of the hidden things, their depth, the perception of springs, of mines, and the boundaries of other matters. As over the width its movement is always uniform, that is to say, that those to whom it turns with a downward movement find a similar movement as long as they walk over the space of the width, and when whilst still walking its movement begins to change, that is, when instead of turning downwards it rises towards the stomach, they know that they enter on the space of the depth, they know, likewise, that they are following the length of a spring, of a mine, or of a limit. When after having seen the movement of lowering over the width, the contrary over the depth, it gives a similar one for the length, that is also in rising against the stomach. Although the third manner of holding the rod does not appear of great utility, because the switch, as we have said, turning indifferently, sometimes on one side, sometimes on the other, it appears as if one cannot so well distinguish the space of the depth of the hidden thing. It has, however, its conveniences, because being neither too much raised, nor too much lowered, its movement is more prompt and more perceptible, when it rises against the stomach, or when it lowers towards the ground, because, having only a quarter of a turn to make in order to rise or fall, it is consequently more easy for it to bend on one side or the other; so that each way of holding the stick has its conveniences, but to use either with success, after having tried them all, it is well to make to oneself a rule to hold it moderately, and always evenly tight, so that one can judge in this equality of the more or of the less of the violence of its movement, otherwise its movement will never be so perceptible, since in one case the violence one does oneself in tightening it too much prevents part of the discernment and sensibility; on the other hand, in not sufficiently tightening the hold, the impression is not so strong, and the movement cannot be so perceptible.

Besides this it is necessary to walk slowly in making this research, for fear the too great activity, or the too large steps, should cause us to perceive the movement only after having passed the place which caused it, and, in losing the place where we ought to dig, we lose by our quickness what we seek with so much care. The form and the different ways of holding the rod make us see the little foundation of those who pretend that it turns in proportion as one places the foot over the hidden thing, inasmuch as it is not only the passing of the body over the thing which gives the movement to the rod, but also that of the rod. This truth can easily be proved in stretching forward the arms of the stick only over the hidden thing and it will be seen that the point will descend or ascend before one or both feet are placed there. What confirms what we have advanced is that the virtue (power) is attached rather to the hands which hold the rod, and which communicate the movement of the blood, than to the other parts of the body which do not touch it. Thus when one says ordinarily that the rod turns in proportion as one puts the foot over the hidden thing, it is an expression which figuratively expresses a part for the whole, or one part for the other. Before finishing this chapter I ought to explain the causes of the different movements of the rod, as well upon the length, as the width, and the depth, but after putting the first in the sixth chapter, before finishing this I will observe that the difference of the movement upon the width and upon the depth is founded upon a natural reason, though its effect does not appear extraordinary, inasmuch as the movement which the rod gives, either above or below, proceeding only as we shall establish presently from subtle bodies of the nature of the hidden thing, which, occupying perpendicularly in the air all its space, attract and cause to bend (by the impression which they give to the blood) the stick towards the place which incloses it as if to indicate it to him. It is not extraordinary that the stick takes a different movement when it leaves the space, because the subtle bodies which it draws with it in leaving it and trying to return to their centre, and being drawn there by the others, or by their natural inclination, cause it to make a circular movement backwards like their own, and consequently different from that they made when they occupied the space. The demonstration of this reason is found in going up or down the course of a spring, because these subtle bodies, being agitated otherwise than they are in crossing it, cause a different movement in the rod.

CHAPTER V.

HOW ONE MAY KNOW IN GENERAL HOW TO DISTINGUISH HIDDEN THINGS BY JACOB'S ROD.

THOSE who seek hidden things often find only as a recompense for their labour and the excessive expense they have made in order to dig, only a piece of stone, of iron, or some metal, instead of the spring they were seeking, and, on the contrary, when wishing for a metal, they find nothing, or a spring so abundant that it would rather inundate than water. This error arises from not knowing the nature of the hidden things, and from not knowing before digging if they are of the quality sought for. It seems at first that this knowledge is impossible, and that unless the earth were of crystal, or that there were a window to look into it, such as an ancient wished in the heart of man, what the former contains is as hidden as the thoughts of the latter are impenetrable. However, experience daily teaches us the contrary, and shows us at the same time that this knowledge is infallible, by observing the things that follow. To be persuaded of it, one must allow two principles, equally incontestable, which will serve as a basis for all discoveries, and as a foundation for all which we shall say. The first that the rod turns over, any hidden thing, of whatever nature it may be, source, mine, metal, mineral, limit, and other things of the kind. The second that apparent things of the same nature take away the movement the one from the other, when seeking them, for example, water, metals, and hidden things give no movement to those of the same nature that are apparent. In a word, the visible thing of the same nature as the hidden one takes away and stops the movement which the rod had over the hidden one. I will give under a separate head the reason of these two principles, and in this I shall prove them by experience. It is certain the rod never turns without a cause, and if in carrying it we find some movement, although we do not at first know the exact material, we ought to conclude that there is a hidden thing in the place where the movement was found. And as the difficulty is to know if it is for water, for a metal, for a limit, or some other hidden thing, we can distinguish and know its nature by applying successively at the end of the rod many different kinds, as gold, silver, copper, lead, a linen or a paper wetted the size of an inch, &c., until we have found the one which stops this movement. Then by the principle which we have established on the subject, you must hold it as certain that the hidden thing is of the same nature, as that which is at the end of the rod, and that the effect ceases by the same cause which produces it. This principle is certain when there is only a single thing hidden capable of producing this movement. But if there are many different ones which cause this movement, we remain always in the same uncertainty, because one kind only does not stop it, when there are others hidden which have the power of moving the rod. For example, a spring flowing in a mine, or in a leaden or brass pipe, will cause the rod to turn, but the mine, lead, copper, or tin in the pipe will do so also, so that the power of the one kind will not stop the movement, whilst there are others which cause it. When, then, we have placed a wet linen rag at the end of the rod it will not cease turning, for the lead, copper, solder or the single pipe, when the spring no longer flows. Therefore we can only discover all these different kinds except by our putting at the end of the rod or in the hollow of the hand, in such a way as that it shall touch them, as many different kinds as may be hidden, such as lead, tin, copper, &c., &c., because then it will stop, and will have no more movement for the reasons we shall name after. It may also occur that at the place of a spring, we may have made a limit, or hidden a treasure. This treasure may be enclosed in a casket, ornamented with nails of iron or of silver, closed with a steel lock, or may be in an earthen vessel, or one of tin, of cast iron, or of metal; it is sure the rod will turn for all these kinds, and that we cannot stop its movement unless by making it touch all at the same time. Which brings me on to say that in order to enlighten oneself truly, we must at first make these experiments for all the kinds individually, and where it is seen that there is not one that stops the rod, touch it with several at once, until its movement is stopped by the influence of all those which are hidden. After seeing the kinds that have stopped it, we ought to conclude, as a natural inference, that there are as many hidden as there were that touched it at the same time. When we have recognised the kind buried, still we do not know its quantity, nor its true quality, if it is a spring or stagnant water, a gold coin or a mine of that metal, a mine or a bar of iron, a mine or a copper coin, &c., and it is not incompatible that all these things, or a good part of them, may be found nearly at the same place. In order to know it, it is only necessary to follow the movement of the rod, whilst ascending and descending, after going over the place cross-wise where the movement was felt; if it is a spring you thus discover the place from whence it springs, and whither it flows, which we could not find in a pond. By this means we distinguish also the piece of metal from the mine, because this last, having veins, or threads, we follow the vein going up and descending, which we cannot do in a piece of metal, bar of iron, or vessel of cast iron, &c., which, having only a limited space, cause the rod to turn in this space, which is never of such an extent as the spring or mine. The way to follow the spring or mine is not difficult, by remarking what we have said in the preceding chapter, that the rod always turns in the same way when one crosses over them, and that it turns differently in returning, or when you go the least from the track. This manner of recognising the mine, or the springs, serves also to distinguish them from other hidden things, for on one side, that over all the rest the rod turns equally, over their length and over their width; and on the other it shows us the difference of the spring which generally only goes on serpentinely, from the limit which goes always straight, and from that which is neither mine nor spring, from that which is, by the little limited space which encloses the first. And though there may be other things almost as extended as the mine, and the subterranean water, as, for example, a source conducted by pipes of lead or other metal, they can also as easily be distinguished by the solderings of the pipes, as by other influences which they have, inasmuch as we cannot stop the movement of the rod upon these solderings or on the other alloys, except by making it touch tin or metals of the same nature as the alloys, which is absolutely useless. When there is only one source or one mine, we can also in the same way distinguish the place where the source loses itself, from that where it is still in the pipe, as water, tin, and lead would be necessary in order to stop it in the place where the pipe is enclosed, and the lead and tin suffice for that where it no longer runs, which is a great help, when one wishes to give up a spring, to avoid digging, and to discover without need other places than that where it fails. All these things are certain and easy to prove, it is only necessary to hide the things over which one desires to experiment, and the truth of what I have advanced will be found. But we must be careful of two things, the first, that he who makes the search does not deprive himself of the power of making the discovery, which may happen to him, if, by example, he have silver buckles, or nails in his shoes, gold rings, &c., or other metals concealed in his clothes, so that the rod would turn to him as easily for what he wore as for the other things hidden.

The second, that the rod must not be of the same nature as the hidden thing, that is to say, of gold, silver, or brass wire, or whalebone, to seek for things of this nature, as it is evident that it would not turn for the same kinds of which it is composed, and this is the case that I have excepted in the second chapter, where I said it turned of whatever material it might be. This also determined me, that it is more sure, and of greater utility, to use one of wood, because the movement of that can never be stopped by another of the same quality. Having removed all that can oppose itself to our intention, he who makes the trial must know two things; the first, that the rod will turn infallibly over the hidden things; the second, that it will stop by the application of a similar matter to the hidden thing.

CHAPTER VI.

HOW TO DISCOVER IN PARTICULAR, MINES AND HIDDEN METALS.

THOUGH in the preceding chapter we have shewn in general the manner of discovering hidden things, and though it seems that what we have said of it ought to give a perfect idea of what to do, still, as there are many particular observations in each kind, which can only be known by long experience, I have thought it necessary to make a special chapter upon what ought to be noticed whilst making the search for metals, mines, and minerals. Those who search for metals would not wish to find water; on the contrary, as it might deceive them in causing the rod to turn, the same as the metal which may be above or under, and may cause them an excessive expense to exhaust it from the mine when it is found with it, they would prefer that there should not be any at all. To extricate one from this embarrassment one tries before every thing to ascertain if there is any spring in the place where the rod turns, and in order to discover it at the time of the search, one has the precaution of putting a wet rag at the end of the rod, and when one sees that this linen does not stop this movement, one knows at once, either that there is no water, or that if there is, it is joined with some other matter that continues this movement. As this matter can only be a metal, a mineral. &c., after having touched it with several metals or minerals, &c., without their stopping, one draws again this conclusion, that there are no metals or minerals, &c., in these places, or that with them there are also other kinds which continue this movement, such as a dead body, a boundary, &c., for a dead body one must touch it with some rotten or putrified animal matter. For limits we will treat of them in another chapter.

It is, then, a certain rule that for the search for metals, one must have the precaution, above all things, 1st, of a wet linen at the end of the rod; 2nd, to furnish oneself with as many different kinds of metals or minerals as one thinks may be contained, and as the virtue of stopping is not affixed to the quantity, but to the quality, one easily judges that the pieces are not likely to be very large, and that it suffices that they are of the weight of a crown of gold; 3rd, one should split the rod with two or three clefts, or more, so that one can put in the clefts the kinds with which one desires to touch it, but for fear that in making these clefts across, the two branches do not separate, you must make them on the side of the branches, and in case one cannot put in all the kinds in the clefts one has made, you can place the rest in the hollow of the hand which touches the rod.

It is also held as a rule that the kinds do not oppose each other, and that when, for example, instead of three kinds that are hidden, one would touch the rod with six, either at the end or in the hand, it is certain that the three superfluous ones will not prevent its movement, as the defect of one of the three could continue it. All that this abundance can produce, is confusion and embarrassment, to know which of the six are not there; to extricate oneself, one must try as often separately and conjointly, that one may find at last the only three which stop it, and at the same time one knows the superfluous ones.

It is also important to remark that if the kinds of which one makes use to stop are not entirely of the same quality as the hidden ones, they will not stop, whence it follows that neither fine gold nor silver will stop for false (inferior), nor the false for the fine (common), tin for fine, nor iron for steel. That is, indeed, very important in this case, when there are two kinds of hidden things in two different places, in order to know in which place is the false, and in which is the real or fine. It appears surprising that steel, which is only a refined iron, does not stop the movement for iron, but the surprise ceases when one remarks that this refinement gives it a different quality, by the aloy which enters into its composition, the same as with the alloy of gold and of silver.

An open mine is a kind of exception to this rule, as much as in the state that it issues from the bosom of the earth, it stops the movement for iron, and iron does so for it, although that seems to imply because the other bodies with which it is still enveloped before being cleansed ought to give it a quality different from iron, nevertheless they produce respectively the same effects, the reason of it is without doubt, that the iron being melted and purified does not change its nature by being freed from the heterogenous substances which enveloped it, like stee, which by its alloy makes a composite of a different nature.

In a word, the iron enveloped by the thick matters of the mine which contains it can arrest the movement on itself, the same as it can upon the mine, but steel ceasing to be iron, by the alloy of which it is composed, the one can no longer arrest the movement of the other. One can extend the consequence of the mine of iron to others of different quality; for example, a piece of silver mine will stop the movement for silver, and silver for the mine, &c., and the same as that steel does not stop the movement for iron; the composition of this metal will not stop the movement for the mine, or the mine for the composition, the same as one may know it by the trial upon fine or inferior silver.

There is still a very curious and necessary observation in the search for mines. It is that there is one part which is so abundant in sulphur and antimony, that they dominate over the metal with which they are mixed. There are other finer ones where the metal dominates over the sulphur and the antimony. In the first kind it might happen that the metal alone could not stop the movement over the mine, because, being, as it were, enveloped in a great abundance of sulphur and antimony, the rod would not turn for the metal alone, therefore one must be provided with a little sulphur and antimony in order to stop its movement; in the second, the metal alone suffices to stop it, which enables us to judge of the fineness (purity) of the mine, because the quantity of the metal exceeds that of the antimony.

Doubtless, it will not be useless to give in this chapter a means of distinguishing springs and mines from other hidden things, of which we have spoken in the preceding chapter. I mean that one may know one is over a spring or mine when, in crossing over it, the rod turns and lowers, and that in rising up again it turns towards the stomach, when one follows the length, which does not happen when there is only one separate metal in the mine, or some other thing enclosed in a limited space, inasmuch as then its movement is always uniform in the length and in the width, and it does not change at all unless one goes out of the space this thing occupies. Here is the reason of this difference, the veins and threads of the mines being affixed to the trunk, like the branches are to the tree, there emanate continually vegetable spirits, which concur in its length to the perfection and to the nourishment of all the parts of this tree. When the man mounts over the space of one of these threads (veins) the subtle parts which emanate from him are drawn by these spirits, and by the shock which they receive from it they are obliged to return to him, and though the man does not feel the movement from it, the rod which receives the impression that these same subtle parts cause him, is obliged to follow their inclination and to return behind like them. One finds the demonstration of this truth in a body which ascends a running stream, inasmuch, as where it is drawn by its movement, or, if it has strength to resist it, it makes in the particles of this element a circular movement around it, which give the same impression to mobile things as are attached to it. But it is not the same with metals separated from the mine, because being in their perfection and separated from the matrix or from the source from which they derived their nourishment, this concourse or this transport of vegetable spirits is no longer made towards them.

It is only the particles or subtle bodies which exhale from themselves that cause the movement of the rod, these subtle bodies exhale equally in all the space which the metals occupy, and produce consequently only an equal movement in the length and in the width. One ought, therefore, to hold the maxims of which we have just spoken as constant (a rule), and it often happens that by wars, and by the lapse of time, by the overturning of edifices, and by inundations, many metals are found enclosed in the bosom of the earth, there will be no difficulty in distinguishing them in the future, if one follows the precepts which we have given, and if in the old and dilapidated or other places believed to enclose something, wet linen does not stop the movement of the rod, one must search in form of a cross over the places where it turns, in order to discover if the movement is different in the width and in the length, and when it is proved to be uniform everywhere, one may boldly conclude that this movement is caused, neither by a spring, nor by a mine, that it must be a metal or some other thing, and afterwards make the different trials of the metals untie you have discovered those that are hidden. For example, if there are arms, the rod will turn equally in the length and in the width of the space which they occupy; but you must not believe that the iron alone stops its movement, as there is steel, others that are ornamented with silver or other metals; to stop the movement you must touch with these metals, and when it stops one can in some measure know their quality, in the same way as one knows their depth in the earth, by what we shall say presently.

It often happens that after having observed all these rules, put the wet rag at the bottom of the rod, and touched it with all these metals in detail, and together, its movement still does not stop, so that one finds oneself in the same doubt (difficulty) as before making the trial. This is the true cause of it; it is that the rod turns also for coal, and for all other minerals, such as mercury, sulphur, antimony, ochre, and their composites in which they dominate, as gypsum, red chalk (not the black, in which there is no cinnabar), and also others, so that if the metals do not suffice to stop the movement, we must again try these minerals and their compositions in any way one can think of, until we has found the one which was wanted to stop the movement. We may then recommence the trial, by taking away one of the kinds which touched besides the last which stopped it, and the rod remaining without movement, we may conclude that there is none of that, and so on consecutively; and when in taking away some one, it is seen to begin to move, you may be sure that there is a similar one hid, and so on successively, until you have taken away all those which do not stop its movement.

CHAPTER VII.

BY WHAT MEANS ONE MAY KNOW THE WIDTH OF THE HIDDEN SPRINGS AND MINES.

I HAVE already stated that the rod turns in descending towards the earth every time one crosses the source or mine, and that when one re-ascends them, and has passed across the space which they occupy, it turns in remounting towards the stomach. This rule will suffice to make us know at first the width of both, but as the knowledge of the width is an indispensable necessity, whether because the large source or mine gives more hope of their abundance, or because one may deceive oneself, because there are mines and sources which, according to the disposition of the land which encloses them, are larger and more abundant in certain pieces than in others, and which extend where there are branches according as it is sandy or mixed with stone, or by the point of a rock. We have been unable to avoid making a separate chapter upon what is necessary to be observed on this point.

The first thing one must observe to well find the width is to hold the rod in the second and third ways, of which we have spoken in the fourth chapter, that is to say, *couchee*, lying or half-lying, whether because in lowering itself easily in this posture it better follows the inclination, whether, also, because by holding it straight, when it would lower, it might turn against the stomach the same as over the length of the source, and thus one might deceive oneself if one did not hold it in one of these two ways which we have named. There is a second observation to make in order to distinguish the source which passes in the sand or gravel from the other kinds mentioned. It is that one must carefully examine if the rod forces equally upon all the width, or if there are places where it forces less than in others. In the last case it is a mark or sign that a part of the source is lost in the gravel or in the sand, and in the first that it is in the rock, or in fuller's earth, which does not permit it to extend itself, which helps much to prevent useless and excessive expense in hollowing (digging) for sources which may be judged from the depth and the aspect of the place to be in the rock. Having observed what is above, you may make the trial upon a bridge. It will be seen that he who passes, walking slowly, and holding the rod in the manner named above, in proportion as he enters, and that he finds himself perpendicularly opposite to the first stone of the arch which touches the water, his rod will begin to turn in lowering its point towards the ground, and will turn always the same until he is at the end of the bridge, perpendicularly opposite to the first stone which touches the water on the other side of the arch. The movement will be different in the rod, and will turn in ascending towards the stomach as if it wished to return or re-unite itself to what it had just left.

One may also make the same trial upon a source conducted through pipes of which one knows the thickness and width. It will be seen that the water which is in these pipes is only at the most three or four inches of width, and that the rod will only turn or lower its point upon crossing for about this space of three or four inches, and if one has not the convenience of a spring in order to make the trial, water may be put into a tub, cover it with a board, and bury it a foot deep, or the depth desired, and, after passing over it with the rod, you will see the same effect as over a bridge, or over a source conducted by pipes. The same trial may be used for metals, and you must only put in the tub a sufficient quantity of them as to cover the bottom, then you will find that the rod will lower over all the space occupied by these metals, after which one may boldly draw this conclusion, that the width of mines and of minerals is to be found in the same way as that of springs. The experience which we have just given of the bridge or of the fountain conducted by pipes, may also serve to teach us to know when we are over the length of springs and mines, inasmuch that after having seen the point of the rod turn in lowering over the width, if we re-mount the spring or the course of a river, we see the rod turning, in re-mounting, against the stomach, which tells us we are over the length by the reasons given in the preceding chapter. Before finishing this one I ought to make some reflections which will indicate to us better the necessity of bringing oneself to well know the width. The first is that there are sources which may be entirely upon the limit of two depths (bottoms), and which will follow them even at whatever running distance, half over one, half over the other, that may happen even in places when one has no

JACOB'S ROD. 37

longer the desire to find them, as it is not permitted to dig on our neighbour's land. Knowing that a part of the width is in ours, we may dig there boldly, and draw there by the opening we make, or by the slant we give, not only the half of the water, but the entire source. The second concerns those to whom the rod turns in proportion as they approach the place which contains the mine or spring, inasmuch as if by a long experience they do not accustom themselves to distinguish the place of his approach of the space they occupy, they would often take the change, and dig in the first instead of the last for sources or metals which they expect to find; they would only have the confusion of having lost their trouble by digging in vain. In order to avoid this, one must consider, first, that in the approach the rod turns almost on all things in an equal distance, and the same on every side across. If by example with sources, or hidden things that are known to us, we remark that in approaching them it turns for two or three feet on each side, we can judge by this distance of that of the things which are not known to us; secondly, that the rod never forces as much in the approach as over the width. There are some, even, who feel only a very little movement from it. On approaching it thus it is not difficult to them to distinguish the place where it does not force from that where it does force; thirdly, we must measure on each side of the mine, or of the source, the distance which is usual to us for the movement of the approach, and after taking the middle, which will be doubtless in the space of the width, and that where the rod joins the most; fourth, in order to assure oneself if this space is that of the width, one must know, that when one ascends or descends a mine or spring, the rod only gives a movement over the true space which they occupy, thus one has only to remount the space which one has marked, and if the rod continues the movement, it is a sure sign one is over the width, and that it is from this place that one ought to seek the depth, as we shall say, afterwards. The third reflexion is for those to whom the rod ordinarily turns in ascending against the stomach, so that if the movement, which is imperfect and irregular, does not appear sufficient to them to indicate the width, there are still means by which they may assure themselves of it, like those of which the movement is irregular. The first is to assure themselves as above, by the two sides of the source or the mine, of the places where the rod forces them least, and to mark with pegs those where the movement begins to be more rapid, and the distance between these two pegs will be that of the width. And if there is none, because that on each side the rapidity of the movement only begins in the same place, or in the place where one has put the first peg, it is a sure sign that the source or mine is very small, or that they are enclosed in this place, since they occupy so little space. The second is, that where the width is found near the first peg, or between the two, to make sure of it, ascend again the mine or source as above, and if the rod gives movement, it is a proof by the rule we have applied to it, that one is over the true width, and thus, in re-ascending the mine or spring, one has only to go out on each side of the space made by the width, and mark there with a peg each extremity where the movement ceased, and the distance of these pegs will again be that of the width; it is a mark the more convincing, if this distance is found to be equal to that of the first two pegs put down. I do not doubt one may have difficulty to know why the rod gives a movement after having crossed the width in a straight line, and why it gives none when one leaves it obliquely, in going up or going down, but this difficulty will cease if you consider that, in the first case, the man who walks in front draws with him certain subtle particles of the source or mine, which wanting to re-unite themselves to those which they have left, continue the movement of the rod by the effort which they make in returning, thus it will be more particularly observed in some other place; but in the second as the man leaves the side, these particles, instead of following him at the moment when he is at the extremity of this width, disperse or glide on and follow the natural inclination of the others.

This truth is clearly demonstrated by those who with a flat rod cross the flames in a straight line, the flat part of the rod being horizontal, by which process the rod is enabled to draw with itself some of the flames for a little space. But, on the contrary, if one were to cross the flames with the rod, the flat part being vertical, none or very little of the particles of the flames would be so drawn. The last reflection we have to make is concerning those to whom the rod only gives movement over certain kinds, and not over all, as they will then make the trials of which we have spoken above. If they do not find what they expected to find they will feel discouraged, and will believe them defective, or that their movement is not sufficient to make discoveries; but that ought not to discourage them, on the contrary, I advise them to assure themselves by many trials of things to which their movement answers, and having found them, to keep only to the discovery of the kinds which are peculiar to them. And amongst those who have this faculty in its perfection, there are almost as many different kinds of movement as of temperaments amongst men. To know the difference of their own from that of others, they should try as much as they can with their friends to whom the rod also gives movement, and by these different trials they will know certainly for which they are fit, and will form for themselves a routine, or a certain habit to use so as usefully to employ their ta ent.

CHAPTER VIII.

BY WHAT MEANS ONE MAY KNOW THE DEPTH OF SOURCES OR METALS.

The knowledge of the width of springs or mines is useless without that of their depth; this last is even of more importance, without it one cannot calculate one's expense with the benefit one expects to receive from the thing whose discovery one desires to make. If the metal is too deep, or in rocks difficult of access, the trouble or the expense may exceed the profit one may receive from its possession. If the spring is not in an elevation proportioned to the incline that we desire, its discovery is more hurtful than profitable to us. We must then necessarily try as much as we can to discover exactly the distance from the depth, and as the preceding chapters have only given us a confused idea of the way to set about it (that is the discovery of springs, mines, &c.) this one will teach the rules that we must use, and the necessary experiences to enlighten us. The first is that when we have found the width of a source or of a mine, and that one know, by the contrary movement that the rod begins to give in ascending towards the stomach, that we are at its extremity, we should mark with a peg the place where this contrary movement began to be felt, and afterwards walk slowly from this peg until we have again remarked that this movement has ceased, or begins to cease. Then mark this place by a second peg, and afterwards one has only to measure from this last to the first, and the depth will be found in the distance which separates them. I mean to say that there will be as many inches, feet, or yards, from the surface of the earth to the place which encloses the hidden thing, as there will be from one peg to another. The second thing necessary to clearly find the depth is to try to assure oneself by some sign that the trial we have just made is not defective. The first is to seek for it on the other side of the width, and to plant there two pegs in the same way in order to see if the distances are equal, which is a true mark of the depth. The second is that we should stop a little in the place where the rod remains motionless, to assure oneself that it has no further movement, and then advance a step or two, and if the rod begins to turn downwards, as over the width, this contrary movement marks infallibly that the place we have just left is that of its depth. The third is that after having advanced seven or eight steps beyond the second peg, we ought to retrace our steps to the first peg planted, and if the space marked is the true width, the rod will remain always motionless until, beginning to pass beyond the first peg planted, we shall enter into the width.

I do not doubt that these signs will surprise many people, but besides the reason of it, which we shall give in another chapter, we may be assured of it by the experience which we have related about it on the bridge, and of a source conducted by pipes. We shall see that as long as we walk upon the bridge holding the rod, in the second or third manner, it will turn towards the earth as we have said, but at the moment we begin to leave the bridge, it will turn ascending towards the stomach, until we are at the distance that there is from the surface of the bridge to the water, after which it will remain without movement, and if having stopped a little in this space we wish to take a step beyond it, the rod will again take its movement for a little time, and this movement will take place as over its width, that is to say, it will turn in lowering itself towards the earth, and if one wishes afterwards to find the exactness of this trial, one has only to take a string, and, after having measured from the surface of the bridge to the water, he will find the same distance from the extremity of the bridge to the first place, where the movement ceased. This demonstration ought to serve for all hidden things. There is, however, this observation to make with regard to sources, that one cannot discern their depth as exactly as we have just remarked inasmuch as the water which passes under a bridge is compressed and limited by the extremities of the arch, but that of springs, besides its ordinary canal, penetrates and moistens also a part of the earth which is at its borders, unless it is in a rock, so that to avoid deceiving oneself in this case we must always augment the distance of the peg by a foot or a foot and a half at the most, according to the size, for more surety; we also make the same augmentation with regard to mines and other hidden things, not only because one never walks so exactly that we cannot miss the space either in advancing too much or too little the foot or the rest of the body, or, also, according as the air is fine or thick, the particles of the body which cause this movement may extend, or remain compressed in their limits. These can, in expanding, give a false movement to the rod before one is over the width, and, without a great experience, they cause us to miss the true place, and, consequently, that of the depth, which one only draws (calculates) upon the extremities of the width, and as this error cannot be considerable, because these particles do not extend very far, it is what has caused us to say that to avoid deceiving oneself we must at the most add a foot or a foot and a half. We have seen in the preceding chapter, when we have spoken of those to whom the rod turns in approaching the hidden thing, a sign that the parts which exhale from the bodies disperse themselves from their true situation, thus I shall not enlarge to enforce the necessity of this augmentation of a foot or a foot and a half, according to the places one has to dig. We must, also, remark that the knowledge of the depth may be interrupted by some mine, some vein, some spring, or some branch which is to be found in the distance which ought to mark it. To enlighten ourselves we must make the experiment on another side. For example, if after the spring or mine which has been found, he has walked for the depth and been interrupted on the side the sun rose, he must retrace his steps, cross the width on the side of its setting, mark the extremity with a peg, and from this place walk slowly until the immobility of the rod causes him to know the depth, and that it is confirmed by his return to the width without any interruption. If we find any again on this side, as it may be only branches of the same spring, or veins of the same mine which are separated, if the place permit it, we must follow one of them going up until we have found the source or trunk, or these two veins, or these two branches united. We can, without obstacle, find the true depth in the manner as above, but if the place does not permit us to follow these branches, as apparently they are of the same depth, we can only find it by planting the first peg at the extremity of the width of the one of those which are at the extremities, and the second at the place where the rod's movement ceases, and afterwards do the same with that which is at the other extremity. If the two distances of depth are found equal we must conclude that this equality is the true sign of it, but if there is some disproportion beyond a foot, it can only be caused by some other spring or by some other branch in the intermediate space, and this it is needful to know in order to gather all the branches, otherwise, as it often happens, we may take only one branch and leave the true and deeper source, and so make useless the measures already taken to make it follow the incline which the branch might have. This is the only means to know the depth in places where the knowledge of it is interrupted by branches of the source, or by veins of a mine, that if this interruption comes from some other hidden thing, such as metal, boundary, &c., you must measure higher or lower from the space which enclosed it, and, by thus doing, be able to find the depth. In a word, in order to well assure oneself of the depth of a source or mine, one must necessarily repass four times its width, that is, once on each side of the source, on the cross in going away from it, and another time, also, on each side on the cross in approaching it, in order to discover if some other branch, or some other hidden thing does not interrupt the discovery of the depth.

It must also be observed, with regard to the depth of mines, that according as the veins or threads are in a straight line, or follow the veins of the earth, or the clefts of the rock which are peculiar to them, it is much less in certain places than in others. For example, a mine whose trunk may be in a mountain, and whose veins go in a straight line, will be much less deep in the two inclines of the mountain than on the top, and, on the contrary, that which follows the veins of the earth, or the clefts of the rock, will be much less deep in the summit than at the two extremities of the mountain, according to the disposition (place) of the said veins. What one ought, also, carefully to observe is following the thread in order by this means to discover the other branches in the event of their being any, and to avoid excessive expense by digging in places thought the most convenient, and where one will find it more largely and more abundant. As to the depth of metals and of other hidden things, it suffices to find the space they occupy, as there is neither thread nor vein to follow, as soon as one has found the place of the movement (of the rod). One can verify it by four different places, that is, from the two extremities of the length, and from the two of the width, and, after having placed a peg at each of these four places, one ought to double each when the contrary movement ceases, and if they are all found in the space which ought to mark the depth, nearly at an equal distance, one may be assured to a foot or about a foot and a half that the hidden thing is in this same distance of depth. If there are many hidden things in the earth in this same space, but some deeper than others, take the distance of the depth the most distant, because in digging they will be found successively one after the other, otherwise one would cease to dig at once at the first kind one might find, thinking there was no more of it, and one might leave the other kinds under or deeper. The rules I have given are certain, and if any one will dig in a place where he believes he has found something, to enlighten himself about it he can before digging hide some metals, or some other thing of the kind, under an arch, in two different places, and, after making the trial himself or by someone else, he will see that he can distinguish the kinds by observing all I have said, the length, and the width they occupy, as well as the depth, but he must take care that in these arches, or under them, there is no iron or other metal affixed, because one well sees that would interrupt his trial, unless he touched the rod with iron or the other metal.

CHAPTER IX.

IF ONE CAN TRULY KNOW THE SIZE OF SOURCES OR OF MINES.

ALMOST all those who attempt to turn the rod, and who believe they have some knowledge of its movement, think to discover nearly the size of a source or that of a mine by the rapidity, or by the slowness of its movement. They think that in the place where it is the quickest and where it forces the most, the source or the mine is there more abundant, and that when it is nearly imperceptible, it is a sign of their smallness and of their sterility. These rules are certain, but they are not conclusive, I mean they are not sufficient to discover exactly the quantity of a source or of a mine. I allow that there are places where the movement is slower than in others, that there are others where the rod turns in spite of the resistance which we can make to it, by tightening it in order to stop it, and that there are others where one can easily stop it, provided one holds it tighter than usual, but that can never serve so as to make known the true quantity of the hidden thing. We can easily judge by the eye, by the knowledge of the land, which may be in a rocky or marshy place, that the source will be more or less abundant, but that serves less to indicate to us the true quantity than a difference of the most or least according as this movement is more or less rapid. In a word, all that one can judge of, is, that there is a certain measure or quantity of material towards which the movement is always slow, and that beyond this measure there is another which renders it everywhere equally rapid, but that demonstrates nothing for the quantity, inasmuch that as soon as the movement attains its rapidity we know less its quantity than its violence, the same as when it is slow, we know less its measure than its slowness. All that can strengthen this opinion, is, that the matter being in small quantity, can only produce few subtle particles, that these few parts can never produce so great an impression as when many are exhaled from an abundant matter. We may judge, then, of the force of this impression by the relation of one to the other, but we can never judge of the most or least of the lightness, nor either of the rapidity, because these subtle parts being as it were imperceptible to one's senses, we can never exactly know the degree of the impression which they give; this knowledge is reserved for Him alone who is the master of the bodies and of the spirits. For example, if we pass over a source of the size of a finger or of an inch and a half, we shall feel a slow movement, not only by the few essences (spirits) which may be in such a little space, but also by the contrariety which is made in the movement of the width with that of the depth, as the passage from the one to the other is imperceptible; the first of the two movements is so also, and is stopped, in some degree, by the last, where the rod finds it before one has scarcely remarked the first. But if we pass over a source as large as the leg, or the arm, there is space enough to perceive the movement of the size, without its being confounded with that of the depth, and we have trouble to arrest the rod's movement, the same as if we pass over a river or a stream, one can make the trial of it. We make the trial of it in passing over the bridge of a river which can be navigated, or over that of an aqueduct or of a stream that turns a windmill, and we shall find everywhere an equally rapid movement. A demonstration may also be made which proves that one does not know exactly the quantity of metals, if, for example, one hides five *louis d'or* in one place, and fifteen in another, when the rod is carried over each of these places, it will force equally without our being able to stop it, although the matter on one side exceeds by three times that of the other, which induces me to conclude that one can never know exactly the degree or the quantity of the hidden things, as also that of the impression which our minds have received, and that at the moment the rod has attained a degree of violence, over a source or over a metal, we know less the quantity of this than the violence of that, as also at the moment it has attained one of slowness, we know rather its slowness than the measure or size of the thing which causes it.

CHAPTER X.

OF THE METHOD OF DISCOVERING BOUNDARIES, ROADS, OR PATHS.

IT is not without reason that the Pagans, who made for themselves Gods, according to their necessities, chose one for limits whom they called the God Termus. There seems something so divine in their formation and in their preservation, the manner of discovering them is so surprising, that it seems at first the human mind wants strength to raise itself to the penetration of the causes which can produce such extraordinary effects. In fact, who could believe it, if daily experience did not teach it to us, that the rod turns over limits the same as over sources and over metals, and that a space which of itself could not give any impression, since by the hand or by man's distinction it has changed place, and been made in order to separate, or bound the estates of two individuals. The very stone seems to animate itself, as well as the space which it occupies in length, and acquires by this destination or planting (forming) a virtue and a quality which it had not before. Yet that is certain, and whilst waiting to relate in some other place the natural reason, we will establish here, according as experience has taught it to us, the rules which we ought to hold in order to discover hidden limits, their depths and the place where they ought to be, when they have been transplanted by the fraud of the proprietors. The first rule that must be observed for the discovery of limits, is that in holding the rod coucheé (lying) or half coucheé, it turns at the moment that we are over the limit, and over the space between two limits, which serve as separation from one limit to the other, when even there shall be no trace to mark it. But it must be observed, that the movement which takes place over the limit, or over the width of the separation, is different from that given over the length. Over the limit or over the width it turns always in lowering, and over the length always in going up towards the stomach, as if one were following a spring, or a vein of a mine. The second is, that the rod turns as well over the visible as over the hidden limit, and not only over the place where it is, but also in that where it ought to be, in the event of its having been transplanted, as well as in all the space that it ought to occupy in length, which indicates and serves to recognise the true place of the separation, when the limit has been changed without the common consent of the proprietors. The third is, that, as metal stops the movement for metal, wet rag for water, &c., so also part of a limit, whether that of the one we seek, or of another, provided it is that of a real limit, or a little of the earth (land) which may be in the space of the length of the limits, stops the movement for limits if you touch them with the rod. So that at the moment that the rod turns in any place, if water, metals, and the other kinds cannot stop its movement, you must touch it with the earth, or with a stone of a limit, and if it stops conclude with certainty that there is a limit in this space, and when you have discovered it you can take away the piece of stone, or of earth, and follow without hindrance the length or the separation which the limit makes, by the movement which the rod will give in mounting towards the stomach, and find the place of its truĕ situation by that it will give in lowering towards the earth. But not to misunderstand the changes in the causes of the movement, we must take the precaution to touch the rod with the other kinds, for fear lest in finding some one, as there may be in the space of the limit, it may cause us to make a deceptive experience, when in order to know it, we would try if the stone or earth from the limit stops the movement, and as there are more springs than other things in the ground, we must consequently take with us a wet rag to put at the end of the rod, lest the water should continue the movement which the boundary earth would stop, the same as you must take with you stone or boundary earth when you seek for a spring or a mine along the boundary, lest the limit continue the movement that the water or the metal would stop. There is a fourth maxim which is curious, in order to discover exactly the separation of the two properties, it is that the rod never turns but over the true limit, or over the true separation. Thus, when the place of the limit has been discovered, by the want of movement, the rod, by touching it with a boundary stone or earth, will show if the limit is in its natural place, or if it has been changed. Inasmuch as if it is truly in the place where the agreement of the parties have placed it, the rod will turn in lowering over the limit, and afterwards it will turn in ascending, during all the space of the length, as far as the other limit, but if it is not in its place, it will turn in lowering over the limit, and will be without movement during all the space of the false length, until the other limit, though there is even a trace between them, and when it passes over the true length, that is to say, over the place which ought to make the true separation, by the first fixing of limits, and by the agreement of the parties, it will turn in lowering when we traverse this length, and in rising towards the stomach when we follow it. And one can only stop it by touching it with the earth of this place or with a boundary stone. This which marks exactly for us the true place of the limit or separation, better than an indifferent stone, or earth which is two or three feet from it, or from that of the false separation, as they could not arrest the movement, like a stone of the limit or earth of the place. One may make proof of these truths, over known limits, and as we have said above, that not only the earth or a piece of stone of the limit we seek stops the movement, but also a piece of a true limit of any place whatever, we can also use this trial over visible boundaries in order to distinguish the true from the false, as over the first the rod turns and its movement cannot be stopped, except by touching it with a stone or earth of the limit, but over the false it never turns whether it touches these things or not, which ought, by the way, to make us admire the Divine Providence, and the goodness of the God of peace, who by an incomprehensible wisdom, has impressed even upon the least things in nature the marks of the principal eulogium which he bears, and such certain signs to preserve it amongst men, that it is not in their power to change a limit without its being known, as we have said above, and as their precautions are so useless against what has been so justly established, if one of them knowing that the rod turns over a true boundary stone, of whatever kind it may be, had taken one from some place in order to transplant it to the place he desired to usurp, his cheating would be known, inasmuch as the rod would truly give movement over this limit, but it would not give it over the separation, or over the length it ought to mark from one boundary to the other. What we have just said is more than sufficient to teach us to find limits, and one can add nothing to it, unless it is that when they are covered, their depth discovers itself in the same way as that of sources, and of mines, and that after having traversed the width of the limits, the contrary movement of the rod ceases at the distance of their depth, the same as with that of sources and of mines. The same Providence which has given the means to know limits, in order to preserve peace amongst men, has also given to us that of knowing the roads (ways) which serve for their communication and society by the same rules, I mean to say, that the rod turns in lowering, when one traverses them, whether they be great roads or paths, and by rising when we follow their length, and in the same way we can only stop it, by causing it to touch a little of the earth of the same road, which ought to be exactly observed, in order not to deceive ourselves, when we seek some source, mine, or metal, in a road, as if the water, or the metal, or the other kinds do not stop the rod, we must make it touch a little of the earth of the road to know if it is not this which causes the continuation of the movement.

CHAPTER XI.

OF THE DIFFERENT CAUSES OF THE ROD'S MOVE-
MENT.

THE movement of the rod is so extraordinary and surprising that one must not be astonished if people reason differently upon the causes which may produce it. Some attribute it to sympathy, and, without teaching us what that is, they explain one difficulty by another still greater, and rather plunge us into than extricate us from our embarrassment. Others treat it as a chimera, and against what experience is continually teaching us, they say that it is false, and that it consists less in a natural action than in a suppleness or dexterity of hands.

There are others, also, who, wanting rather penetration than knowledge in physical and natural causes, attribute it to sorcery, to Satan, or to the spirits of the air, all which is beyond their understanding, and, without considering that it is not a less sin to accuse the work of the Great Architect of imperfection, than to have recourse without necessity to spiritual intelligences in order to supply (aid) these pretended imperfections. They have recourse to spirits, though they themselves forbid access to them, and as the knowledge of them is still more difficult than of that which they neglect to know, they can without trouble attribute to them all the functions of which they stand in need to support their opinion, and by favour of the different operations which they attribute to them, withdraw themselves from the embarrassment into which their negligence has put them. Upon this principle they say, first, that this movement is supernatural, and, without examining, that it is always equal, that its effect does not vary, and that loadstone not better attracts iron, heavy things tend not less to fall, nor the lighter ones to ascend, than that the rod turns when one is over a spring or a mine, they boldly sustain that the devil has to do with it, and although he is the most unhappy of all creatures, they do him the honor to attribute to him an effect which is only the work of Divinity. Besides, there is no one who does not agree that the operations of spirits dependent upon a changeable will are inconstant and subject to change like it, and as they act rather by caprice than by necessity, their operations are always diverse, which one never finds in those of nature. Loadstone has always attracted iron; fire has always tended upwards; earth has always fallen downwards; and the rod has always turned when it has been carried over matter proper to cause its movement. I maintain, therefore, that there is nothing in the movement of the rod that physical causes cannot attain (or explain), and if one will penetrate them without prejudice or a preformed opinion, without seeing its consequences, or without sheltering oneself under favour of a little knowledge of supernatural causes, we shall discover three things. The first, that if this movement were caused by the spirits of the air it could only be by virtue of an expressed or tacit agreement. This rod turns with children, with persons so pious that one could not, without crime, accuse them with an agreement with the devil. One can less accuse them of a tacit one, because, in renouncing it with all their heart, as if needful they would no doubt do, it would remain without effect, and the movement of the rod would cease, which it never does whether they renounce or not. The second is, that if the devil had to do with it the rod would turn with every one, for there would be no reason to cause him to prefer some to others, and yet we see that there is more than the half, perhaps three quarters, with whom it does not produce this effect. The third thing they will discover is, that there is nothing imperfect in nature, that all bodies have means or natural signs which cause them to be known inwardly. The leaf and the bark of the tree are the marks of its species, the flower is that of the fruit it ought to bear, and the branches and the trunk are those of the roots which are hidden. All these different things being borne to the exterior senses of men by the kinds which emanate from them, subordinately serve to make him distinguish them, the same as the impression that the interior senses receive for hidden things serves to make him know them by the movement of the rod. These two kinds of knowledge have not a more supernatural sensation the one than the other, and, unless by attributing still to the spirits of the air that which we have of plants and of other bodies of nature, one cannot give them the direction of that which we receive from the movement of the rod. To make this truth plain one must lay down some rules which in good philosophy will not be contested. The first is, that there emanates or exhales generally from all bodies some subtle particles, which with good reason might be called spirits if they did not come from matter. Corporeal would not need sustenance for their individual support, if it were not necessary for them to avoid their total ruin by repairing the breaches made by this continual emanation. Without these particles the vapours or exhalations could not be formed, the mirror would reflect no species of things, the light would not communicate itself to our eyes, the odour of flowers would not convey itself to our sense of smell, the dog would not discover the scent of the game, the trace of his master, or would not choose a stone which he had thrown into a heap from others, or into the water. In fine, it is only by these particles that plants draw their nourishment, that amber attracts straw, loadstone iron, and that we distinguish the kind from which they emanate, and it would be purposeless to enquire why they do not attract all kinds, like the loadstone, &c., for some having more activity than others, according to the ruling or composed matter from which they emanate, they find themselves, consequently, more or less active. Loadstone, for instance, or straw, would have more air or more fire, which causes a grea'er activity in their particles, so with the rest. The second rule we must observe is, that these subtle particles reside and fly about perpetually in the air, around the matter from which they are emanated, and, according to its superficies, like a smoke which whirls over a fire, or a fog over water, so that though agitated by a slight movement, they are in a perpetual repose in this place, the same as the parts of a running water which are in its bed, or of a fire which is not agitated by a wind, or by some other bodies are said to be in repose. The third, that this repose is never disturbed except by the interjection of another body, which, mixing itself with them, receives the communication of their kind by the agitation or by the impression which they give to it in joining themselves to it. It is thus that those who go upon water feel the damp, and in some way become damp by the particles of water which surround them. It is thus, also, that he who walks in a dry, barren place, filled with sulphur, or with some other mineral, will feel the sulphur, bitumen, or any other burnt thing by the touch, or by the junction of the subtle particles which exhale from these bodies. In fine, it is thus that our hair stands on end, and that we have a horror when we pass through a place where a man has been killed, or where his corpse has been buried. In the fourth place, we must remark that of the agitations which happen to these particles some are ordinary by the simple interposition of the bodies, the others extraordinary, which proceed from the separation of these particles from their common matrix, or from the matter from which they emanated. The first of these agitations is light, and produces only the simple feeling, the second is violent, and is much more sensible. Fire never acts with more violence than when in blowing it you separate it from its aliment. A torrent is never more impetuous nor more rapid than when barriers are opposed to its passage; heavy things never tend more violently downwards than when they are the most raised, nor light ones upwards than when they are the lowest; in the same way these particles never tend more to their centre, or to re-unite themselves to their common matrix, than when they are the most separated from it, and their impression is never more violent than when they concentrate themselves to return to it. From all these rules we gather a fifth; it is that the sensation or the distinction which we make of the kinds is only made by the impression which the blood receives from these particles or by the rapport which those which emanate from us make to it from the meeting (mixture) which they have made with those of other kinds. And thus, how these foreign particles touching those which emanate from us, and repulsing them, impress them with their movement, and, joining themselves to them, carry away their distinction from our imagination by the difference which it finds in their movement. It is then certain that it is by the movement of these subtle bodies, and by the impression which their touch gives to those which emanate from us, that the sensation or the distinction of kinds is made, that the imagination recognises them according to the manner by which it is struck by these particles, and to give it the knowledge of them it is requisite, necessarily, that the communication or touch of two opposite bodies gives or impresses on it a specific movement. There is no one who does not allow that these rules are natural. One may believe them without begging the assistance of spiritual intelligences to perform these operations. One will believe thus, that it is in this manner one knows the species of a tree by the subtle particles of the flower, the leaf and the bark, and that we judge that its roots are hidden by the branches and the trunk which are over, and, in fine, that there is something hidden in the earth by the impression given by the particles which are over it. This is how I prove it, when we walk in some place where there is something hidden, the impression which our subtle parts receive from those which occupy the space of the surface of the mines, sources, metals, &c., obliges those which have emanated from our bodies to re-enter our blood tumultuously, to give of them, according to custom, the rapport to the imagination by the difference of the movement. Why should it not be, that in proportion as these particles enter tumultuously into the body of the man in order to mark their impression to him they should cause to go out from him others of which they take the place, which insinuating themselves by the pores into the rod communicate to it the movement which they have just received. This is the true cause of the movement; it is from the shock or from this impression, which lasts as long as one occupies the space of these heterogeneous bodies, that the turning of the rod comes, and one may boldly assert that as the quickening or the lowering of the pulse marks the different passions by which our blood is affected, the movement of the rod is like a second pulse which marks the agitation our minds have received by the shock of foreign substances, and if we see that, generally, certain maladies are taken through having drunk from the same glass or by the simple touch, the furies of a mad animal by its saliva or by its bite, that love as well as disease of the eyes by a fixed look, and that there are even animals and certain persons who infect certain objects by their looks why should it not be that by a man's touch of the rod he should communicate to it the impression that his blood has just received from the shock caused by the particles of the hidden thing. I shall, doubtless, be asked two things, from whence comes it that these particles which enter into the body, and which give the movement to the rod, do not make themselves known to the imagination, when the species is hidden, the same as when it is apparent; for example, why the kinds of hidden gold do not make it known to our imagination by the difference of their movement the same as when it is discovered. The knot of this objection resolves itself by the principles we have placed above, inasmuch as when the kind is apparent it strikes the exterior sense with an ordinary movement, a natural one, which makes, according to its custom, the rapport to the interior sense, which knows it by this rapport, but when the kind is hidden, as the particles which emanate from it no longer strike the exterior senses, and only give an ordinary movement to the interior, or contrary to the natural, it follows that they can no longer, by this movement, carry the distinction of the kinds which produces them, as, for example, supposing the ordinary movement was high or oblique, the extraordinary would be low or towards the hidden thing to which these particles tend to reunite themselves. This contrariety of movement prevents it producing the same effect. In a word, when the kind is apparent, the subtle particles which emanate from it having only their ordinary movement, the imagination can easily distinguish them by the rapport of the exterior senses which is struck by it,

JACOB'S ROD. 63

but when it is hidden the movement of these particles being changed by the interjection of the body which covers them, and from the ordinary become extraordinary, or, contrary to the na ural, it no longer affects the same the exterior sense, and if it affects the interior it is a movement which is unknown to it, as proceeding from a strange sound of which it does not understand the language.

The second objection which will be made to me will be, w iy this impression does not produce the same effect on all men, or why the rod does not turn to every one equally. I reply to that, that in the same way there are lands naturally sterile, and others naturally fertile, according to the different aspects of the sun, or of other planets, healthy and unhealthy air, according as they are filled with particles conformable or contrary to the temperature of the bodies submitted to them, and pure or impure air according as they are laden or out of the sphere of these different particles, so there are bodies which abound in these subtle parts, and others which have scarcely enough of them, besides that there are some which have them more active than others, and which have the pores extremely open, others which have them very closed. Those who are born under certain signs or planets, may have these particles so abundant and so active, and the pores so open, that, being repulsed by foreign ones, they must necessarily issue by the pores to make place for those which enter our bodies when we breathe, inasmuch as the vessel being filled neither can remain, and the facility or impetuosity with which they go out commùuicates or impresses their movement to the rod, but those whose pores are closer, or who have not these particles neither so abundant nor active, that others can only enter by obliging those that are there to go out and give them place, cannot impress on the rod the movement they have received, because those outside have not so strong an agitation as those inside, or do not feel it. Here is then the effect the sign or planet produces; it is that it opens the pores of some, and gives them a great abundance of these most active particles, that on the least impression they go out to give place to those sent by foreign bodies, and to others where it gives less activity to their subtle parts, or so closes their pores that this transpiration cannot be made, or if the pores are tortuous, it causes the movement not to be regular, but always in turning upwards towards the stomach or in lowering towards the earth. From thence it is that there are some who have this movement for all hidden things, and others only for some, because if they have the pores very open and straight, this abundance of particles, with the required activity, the rod will turn to them without doubt upon all kinds, but if they have only a plentitude of particles, with closed pores, there will only be a movement for what gives them the strongest impression, or which accomodates itself the most to their temperament, and thus, in proportion as the activity or plentitude is wanting to these particles, or that the pores are more or less closed. I boldly, then, draw this conclusion, that, without having recourse to spiritual intelligences, one may ho d it as certain that the movement of the rod is physical, that it proceeds only from a physical cause, that is to say, from our particles which emanate from us, upon the shock they receive from foreign ones, which communicate to the rod the impression they have received from them.

CHAPTER XII.

EXPLANATION OF SOME DOUBTS UPON THE CAUSES OF THE ROD'S MOVEMENT.

THE most palpable truth is always contested, and it is generally in dispute and opposition that it shines, and that it appears with most brilliancy. The principles we have laid down in the preceding chapter are certain, but they are not without some difficulties. We will try to resolve them in this, and to put them as in a new light, by the opposition of contrary reasons. There are few persons who contest the emanation of subtle bodies, and who do not allow that they give some impression to our senses, but they cannot understand how by this impression we can know the space or width of the hidden things, their depth, to distinguish the different kinds, to know the concealed thing, the criminal, or boundaries, and here are the reasons upon which they may conceive it as we ourselves can. I have established as a rule that at the moment one passes over the width of the hidden thing, the rod gives a movement lowering itself. The penetration of the cause is not difficult, the subtle parts which excite this movement being separated from their centre or from their common matrix, push each other, and generally tend towards it to re-unite themselves, and, being met by those of the man who crosses them, in proportion as he enters into the space they occupy, they impress upon them the same movement that these communicate afterwards to the rod, and as their movement is downwards or towards the thing concealed, they make it do the same, and give it the same inflexion at the end (where, or), re-uniting themselves, as it has been said before. They have, consequently, more strength in this place to mark it. From thence one discovers at the same time the cause of the rapidity or of the slowness of this movement, inasmuch as at the places where there is the most matter causing a great shock, and a great escape of these subtle parts, they consequently cause a more rapid movement than when there is very little. A little rivulet has never as much rapidity and impetuosity as a torrent, and one more easily extinguishes a little light than a fire. One ought not, then, to be astonished if in judging of the place, or of the abundance of a spring, and of that which is only imbibed, because what has been said makes us see how the last ought to give a slower movement than the first. The foundation or rule I have laid down regarding the depth is that it is marked by the movement which the rod gives in mounting against the stomach from the width, until the movement ceases, and that after having ceased, if one advances a step, it gives a contrary movement below. The causes of these effects are nearly similar to those of the preceding, because the subtle particles which produce them being drawn by the body which has traversed them, beyond the space which they occupied, they take a movement behind in order to arrive at the place from which they have been drawn, and, consequently, give the same to the particles of the man, and successively to the rod, which they also cause to turn backwards, that is to say, in ascending towards the stomach, and as these particles cannot act beyond the sphere of their activity, this sphere only extending itself to the distance of the intermediate body, that is to say, for example, the ground which separates them, their movement ceasing in this interval, one knows, consequently, the distance of the depth. The solution of this difficulty serves also to show us how it happens that these particles give the same movement when one ascends a source or mine, because these subtle bodies, following the bent of that from which they emanate, in which they mix and float perpetually from one extremity to the other, being stopped and agitated by the body which opposes itself to their passage, and which crosses them, make a circular movement around it, in order to re-take their natural bent, like the parts of water or of fire which are stopped by a b dy, and this is what causes a backward movement, rising against the stomach, as it has been said elsewhere. There still remains a difficulty about the depth, it is how it happens that after the movement which marks its distance has ceased, if one advances still a step, it re-takes a contrary movement, that is, lowering, and that afterwards, if one retraces one's steps, it gives none at all until one has again entered into the width. This difficulty will cease when one comes to think that the want of movement which happens to the rod at the extremity of the distance of the depth only proceeds from the absence of the subtle particles which caused it, because, having withdrawn themselves, the rod can no longer have the backward movement which it received by their impression, and if in passing beyond by a step the place where this movement has ceased, it comes to give a contrary one. It is not through having received a new impression from particles different to the first which agitated it, but rather because there still remain some, which, not having been able, like the others, to return, cause the rod to turn by the new effort which they make to rejoin them, and as they are no longer drawn behind by the rapidity of their movement, they follow, and cause the rod to follow their ordinary bent, which is to tend downwards. One sees the demonstration of this truth in those who go out of a place full of thick smoke, or in those who go out of water, they draw with them an abundance of smoke, or of water, which follows them for some space, not always as much as these particles because it is heavier, but at least enough to cause us to comprehend that when the smoke or the water which accompanied the body went out from it, has retired into its place or its channel, there always remain some parts or some drops attached to the body, which, not having so well been able to be separated from it as the others, no longer tend towards the mass they have left, but upwards or below, where they go successively according to their bent and natural inclination, and the same that after this water has run off until it has rejoined the mass or the stream, one feels no dampness, because no part of the water remains upon him; the same also when one returns upon the depth after leaving it for a few steps, when one traverses it the rod gives no movement until he begins to enter into the width, because all these particles being entirely withdrawn they give no impression until they are rejoined in the current, that is to say, in the space which they occupy over the width. As to the distinction of kinds, I have established, as a rule, that one knows them in this, that at the moment of their touching the rod with substances of the same nature as the hidden thing, its movement is arrested. The cause of this effect is as evident as that of the preceding, because the kind which touches or which appears, attracting or re-uniting to itself these particles (which, by the total separation from their centre, or from their common matrix, were in a violent agitation to re-unite themselves to it) puts them into repose and causes their agitation to cease by their re-union to the kind of the same nature that they touch on the rod. It is thus that the magnetic needle, which naturally turns itself towards the side of the North Pole, where the centre of attraction is, stops its movement and ceases to turn. The movement or the extraordinary agitation which these subtle bodies had by their separation from their centre being thus stopped, there only remains the natural or ordinary, which, by itself, giving no impression, or a very light one, as being in repose, or re-united to a matter of the same quality as that from which they were separated. One ought not to be astonished that the rod does not turn over water, nor over all the other visible kinds, because the particles of water, &c., being in repose, give no impression to the body which they surround, or only give it one so light that it is imperceptible, as we have said. A proof that these particles give no impression when they are in the place of their repose, is that their activity only proceeds from the violence which they feel when they are separated from it. We do not smell the odour of a flower if we do not draw its particles in breathing; our respiration must draw them with violence to our smell; a dog would not find the scent of game, nor that of his master, if respiration did not draw it; and thus with the rest, so that these particles do not give any sensible impression if the violence they suffer does not excite them and give them activity. Still they say, supposing it to be so, how shall one know the place where a stolen thing has been hidden, or the thief, or the criminal; it appears that the difficulty no longer exists for the stolen thing, because, being a body, as well as the other kinds of which we have spoken, it can exhale particles which may give impression or movement to the rod, which one may stop and know the cause of by touching it with things of the same kind if one has them, so that, if after having touched it, it continues its movement, one may say the same as with the sources, that this continuation proceeds from another cause, which may by chance be found in the place where one seeks. But that does not suffice to discover if the thing has been stolen or not, because it may be that the rod turns less for the theft than for the thing stolen. Yet, as we are convinced that the rod turns equally over the criminal, and over the stolen thing, after having verified for more certainty that there is no foreign cause for its movement, I no longer doubt that the crime affects the thing and the criminal with a particular quality which they had not before, and that the agitation which remorse excites in the particles of the criminal since the crime was committed is redoubled by their union to those of the stolen thing, and that this union, like that which takes place over limits (as we shall afterwards show), makes a composition which perpetuates a uniform movement to the rod in every place where the thief has passed or the stolen thing, and principally in those where either has stopped, so that nothing can stop its movement over either, because when it is touched with similar things they would not be affected by a similar union or a similar quality of theft. What confirms me in the belief of this union is that the more abundant are the subtle particles of the thing which has given rise to the crime, the more violent is the impression which they give. For example, the union of the particles of the murderer with those of the murdered would give a greater impression than those of the thief with those of the stolen thing, because in the first case there is a greater and more violent exhalation from the particles of the murdered, and as they are stronger I do not doubt that they follow everywhere those of the murderer, and that the movement which they excite is still stronger for the knowledge of this crime than that which is excited by simple theft. This truth is also proved by the movement which the rod gives to the places where the criminal or the thing affected by the crime are lying, inasmuch as that there is there a greater exhalation of these particles, the rod consequently gives more movement, which causes the place to be easily known, and by this reason one also easily knows the place where the crime has been committed, because, as there is there a greater exhalation, the movement is also more rapid. In a word, if, as is said, the rod turns over all criminals, of whatever nature the crime, this movement only proceeds from a similar union, or from that since the crime committed, the subtle particles of the criminals being more than usually agitated, they have taken a movement differing from those of the innocent, which causes that being more violent, it suffices to move the rod of him who seeks. But as a jury decides that for conviction there should be proofs clearer than the day, I would not at once trust to this, not only because I may fail to touch the rod with some kind which, stopping its movement, would discharge the criminal of the crime laid to him, but also because a man, agitated by an ill-founded fear, or by some imagination in his head, might cause the same movement; the same as a man firm, without remorse and without fear, although the criminal giving no agitation to his spirits could not give any to the rod, which can, however, happen with difficulty, because the said union is always to the last, and is wanting to the first. Yet in a case of crime one must always lean to the gentlest side. I resolve to say that its movement over a criminal can never serve as a proof for his conviction, but only for some indication or presumption of it. The last difficulty which remains to be examined concerns the movement of the rod over limits. I agree that there are things which appear to surpass physical causes. One finds it difficult to think that a stone, which of itself gives no movement, can give one at the moment where it is employed for limits, and that a space which from its nature gives none, as soon as it

JACOB'S ROD. 73

is employed to make the separation of some property, begins to enclose in itself animated particles which cause this movement, yet experience shows it us every day, and teaches us at the same time, that besides the will of God, which has disposed all things by its providence in such sort as to keep peace amongst men. This effect is produced in the same way as the preceding over water, minerals, &c. In a word, it is by the means of the common subtle kinds (fluids) in the body which are exhaled from the surrounding parts when they planted the limits. No one disallows that in this movement the two interested parties, or some one for them were there, that these parties having agreed on the space which ought to make the separation, and the place were the limits ought to be planted, would go and return along this separation in order to place the cords and pegs, and shed in this planting, or in these alleys and paths, a quantity of those particles or subtle bodies which cause the movement, and that they shed still more in touching the stones which serve as a limit, and that, in proportion as they bury these stones, they bury a quantity of these particles with them. It is these particles of different kinds which make a union, which reproduces continually similar ones to their composition. It is these buried particles or subtle bodies, which, by Divine permission, compose a kind of mass or circle of them, which keep as enchained or attached to them by an invisible chain those which remain in the air all along the path traced by them during the space of the separation. It is these last, which moving and reproducing themselves perpetually in this space from one limit to another, as to the place of their attachment give and impress on the rod a movement similar to that which it has over sources and mines. It appears that I see a crowd of opponents who would ask me how it is that these particles are not exhaled by the succession of time, but I answer that that ought not to appear more strange to them than to see the mistletoe of the oak or apple tree, which they pretend grows from the excrement of a bird, produce itself, generate, and remain perpetually upon the matter on which this excrement fell, spite of sun, and wind, and rain. Moreover, it is not more surprising to see the particles perpetually remaining over the limits, and reproducing themselves than to see (according to what naturalists say) that one of the drops of milk which issues from coral (when broken in the sea) produce there another coral shrub upon whatever it falls, and that this drop, without varying, rests on the place where it falls, produces there a new coral branch, brings it up, and causes it to grow as large or larger as that from which it was produced, spite of the agitation of the waves and the movement of the water, which ought as easily to carry this drop of milk above the stone or place where it falls, impede its generation, and prevent its reproducing itself, as the winds or succession of time can carry away the particles of the surrounding parties, which are sown upon the limit or upon the space of the separation. In fine, one ought no more to be astonished to see these particles fixed upon limits, or upon the space of separation than at what we remember for sixty or eighty or more years, things that we have seen, felt, tasted, touched, &c. There are few philosophers who do not agree that this reminiscence is caused by means of particles, which, remaining attached to our senses, although the object is no longer there, by recalling the idea of it to our memory every time they represent themselves to our imagination. Why not allow the same with particles buried with limits, perpetually remaining there, that they reproduce it, and, being of the same nature as those in the air, in the space of separation, they keep them there attached like a tree which is upon its root, or by the inclination which they have to re-unite with their like, and make them remain there, so that they present tnemselves to the man the same as the intentional kinds to memory; the reason is the same for both. It is certain that these particles, or those which are reproduced by them, remain about these limits, either flying about or running continually from one limit to another, or all along the separation where they are seen, they tend downwards continually towards those which are attached to the limits, which causes a similar movement to the rod when one traverses them, as that which it receives in traversing a source or a mine, and a contrary one when in following the length one opposes their passage, the same as one sees a contrary one when in ascending a source or vein of a mine, one opposes the passage of the particles which are following their bent. One will object, that if this movement is similar to that made over mines, springs, &c., why does the rod turn upon the visible stone of limit, and not over water or the matter of the mine. This difficulty can be resolved, but to make it more clear I shall observe three things, the first that the particles emanated from surrounding parties, which are enclosed with the limits are so united in them, that they may be said to be concentrated; the second, that the superficies of the apparent limit, like that of the ground of separation, have no part in this re-union, the same as the surface of the man has no part in the kinds which he encloses in himself. The third, that the traces which the parties have made in going and coming along the separation have also concentrated some which are like the stem, or root, or centre of those which circulate in the air above this place. This agreed, one easily discovers why the apparent limit or ground of separation cannot arrest the movement of the rod, for being only a surface, which is not like what they enclose of the same nature as the particles in the air, and which have caused the movement, they can neither stop it nor cause it to cease, because they do not stop their agitation in re-uniting and in putting them into the repose they seek as the spring or apparent mine do to the subtle bodies of similar natures to themselves, and if in breaking a piece of the boundary stone, or lump of earth from the separation line, they stop the movement, it is that in breaking these pieces some of those particles which were concentrated are discovered, which, by the touch of the rod, re-uniting the others to them, and putting them into the repose they sought, cause their agitation to cease, and consequently arrest the movement which they caused. This reason serves also to teach us how it is that when a limit is changed the rod does not turn over the false length, because the subtle particles which were concentrated in the true separation have not quitted it to follow the limit when it was changed, and it turns always over the true separation, or over the limit where they were concentrated, rather than over the false separation, because none of these concentrated particles, being in this place those which are in the air are not attracted as over the true separation, where some always remain concentrated, to which they try to re-unite themselves. Doubtless, the rules I have given about the planting of limits will make some say I have gone beyond those of reason, but I shall be glad if they can contradict me without doing so, and until beyond the causes that I attribute to the will and power of God, which are beyond limit, let him give me more natural or apparent causes than mine. I declare that rather than have recourse to the spirits of the air I shall keep to my first opinion, which, being founded on a physical and real cause, produces always the same effect, which would not be found in the spirits of the air, or by spiritual intelligences, and, by this means, instead of taxing with imperfection the work of the Creator, I praise and admire incessantly the Great Workman, who, by an operation of which He alone is capable, has shewn in the least things the signs of His goodness toward man.

FINIS.

ADDENDA.

CHAPTER I.

IF further proof be needed of the existence of the faculty of finding minerals, &c., I cannot do better than quote largely from the volumes of the *Spiritual Magazine*, as by so doing a much more comprehensive view of the subject will be obtained, with the experiences of others also, some of high rank and well known, premising however that the quotations have been copied from other works.

This I do that no doubt may remain on the mind as to their truth, and to prove, as far as testimony will do so, their correctness, and as the works are now scarce and expensive, it will save the trouble of procuring them.

DIVINING RODS AND HAZEL WANDS.
Spiritual Magazine, March, 1862.

IT is grateful to us to have to quote again from the pages of *All the Year Round*, some excellent remarks by Mr. Dickens' great collaborateur, Sir E. Bulwer Lytton, on this subject. Neither divining rods nor hazel wands have been much heard of as forming part of the modern manifestions. As for divining rods, they are, with the exception of those mentioned in the Bible, almost entirely connected in our minds with the magical arts of the earlier and middle ages, and they have disappeared from amongst us, who are seeking rather to develope Spiritualism as an incident of higher laws, than to cultivate the supposed relations of the magician. Hazel wands, on the contrary, have been more heard of, for no such uncanny ideas attached to them, for they have been carried to advantage in the hands of sickly girls, and others of the magnetic temperament, in searching successfully for mines and springs of water. The hazel wand performed wonders in the hands of Angelique Cottin. Indeed, its use has been occassional for many years in England also. We know that the well known Mr. Cookworthy, the Swedenborgian, and the father of English pottery, used it with remarkable success in prospecting for the celebrated china clay found by him in Cornwall. We also know a lady now in London who has a somewhat analogous though more spiritual power, and who, while in London on one occasion, without the hazel wand, detected, by merely passing her hand over the plan of an estate situate near Reigate, the exact spot on which water would be found, stating at the same time that the sinking then being made was in the wrong place. Both her statements were found to be true. Water was found with n twelve feet of the surface where she indicated it, after a large expenditure had been made in continuing the other sinking to a great depth without success.

There is no doubt also that, as in the case of the planchette, some woods and materials are better adapted than others for collecting and retaining the magnetic properties, communicated through the human spirit. For the planchette, sandal wood has been mentioned as the best. How it has come to select the hazel we know not, excepting that the wood is common and handy for the purpose, or that its use is like much of our wisdom, the result of tradition, the origin of which is lost.

Sir Bulwer Lytton is able to quote Bacon, the great Master of Philosophy, on this interesting subject. It is not long since Sir W. Page Wood, in delivering a lecture at Exeter Hall, introduced the subject of the spiritual phenomena, and with the most contemptuous sneer, asked " Could such things be in the country of Bacon, and in the nineteenth century?" "Yes," we say to the Vice-Chancellor, "such things can be, and are in the country of Bacon; and if you had known Bacon better, you would have found that his belief and his philosophy were both in favour of what you denied." We have shewn this in quotations from the works of the great philosopher in our very first number, and we agree with Sir Bulwer Lytton, who says for the benefit of Sir W. Page Wood, Mr. Dickens, and others of that stamp, "Lord Bacon, were he now living, *would be the man to solve the mysteries that branch out of mesmerism, or (so called) spiritual manifestation, for he would not pretend to despise their phenomena for fear of hurting his reputation for good sense;*" and Bacon is quoted by Sir Bulwer Lytton, suggesting " that there be many things, some of them inanimate, that operate upon the spirits of men by secret sympathy and antipathy," and to which Bacon gives the quaint name of "imaginants;" and Sir Bulwer adds, " so even that wand, of which I have described to you the magic-like effects, may have had properties communicated to it, by which it performs the work of the magician, as mesmerists pretend that some substance mesmerized by them can act on the patient as sensibly as if it were the mesmerizer himself." "And," says Bacon earnestly, in a very different spirit from that which dictates to the sages of our time the philosophy of rejecting without trial that which belongs to the marvellous—"*and whatsoever is of this kind, should be thoroughly enquired into ;*" and this great founder or renovator of the sober inductive system of investigation, even so far leaves it a matter of speculative enquiry, whether imagination may not be so powerful that it can actually create upon a plant, that he says, "This likewise should be made upon plants, and that diligently, as if you should tell a man that such a tree would die this year, and *will* him, at these and these times, to go unto it and see how it thriveth." I presume that no philosopher has followed such recommendations. Had some real philosopher done so, possibly we should by this time know all the secrets of what is popularly called witchcraft.

Sir Bulwer Lytton proceeds :

"May it not be possible, apart from the doubtful question whether a man can communicate to an inanimate material substance, a power to act upon the mind or imagination of another man—may it not, I say, be possible that such a substance may contain in itself such a virtue or property, potent over certain constitutions, though not over all? For instance, it is in my experience that the common hazel-wood will strongly affect some nervous temperaments, though wholly without effects on others. I remember a young girl who, having taken up a hazel stick freshly cut, could not relax her hold of it ; and when it was wrenched away from her by force, was irresistibly attracted towards it, repossessed herself of it, and, after holding it a few minutes, was cast into a kind of trance in which she beheld phantasmal visions. Mentioning this curious case, which I supposed unique, to a learned brother of our profession, he told me that he had known other instances of the effect of the hazel upon nervous temperaments in persons of both sexes. Possibly it was some such peculiar property in the hazel that made it the wood selected for the old divining rod. Again, we know that the bay-tree or laurel was dedicated to the oracular Pythan Apollo. Now, wherever in the old world we find that the learning of the priests enabled them to exhibit exceptional phenomena, which imposed upon popular credulity, there was something or other which it is worth a philosopher's while to explore. And, accordingly, I always suspected that there was in the laurel some property favourable to ecstatic vision, in highly impressionable temperaments. My suspicion, a few years ago, was justified by the experience of a German physician, who had under his care a cataleptic or ecstatic patient, and who assured me, that he found nothing in this patient, so stimulated the state of 'sleep-waking,' or so disposed that state to indulge in the hallucinations of previsions, as the berry of the laurel.* Well, we do not know what this wand, that produced a seemingly magical effect upon you, was really composed of. You did not notice the metal employed in the wire, which you say communicated a thrill to the sensitive nerves in the palm of the hand. You cannot tell how far it may have been the vehicle of some fluid force in nature. Or, still more probably, whether the pores of your hand insensibly imbibed, and communicated to to the brain, some of those powerful narcotics, from which the Budhists and Arabs make unguents that induce visionary hallucinations, and in which substances undetected in the hollow of the wand, or the handle of the wand itself, might be steeped.† One thing we do know, *viz.*, that amongst the ancients, and especially in the East, the construction of wands for magical purposes, was no common-place mechanical craft, but a special and secret art appropriated to men, who culivated, with assiduity all that was then known of natural science, in order to extract from it agencies what might appear supernatural. Possibly then, the rods or wands of the East, and of which Scripture makes mention, were framed upon some principles of which we in our day are very naturally ignorant, since we do not ransack science for the same secrets. And thus in the selection or preparations of the material employed, mainly consisted whatever may be referable to natural philosophical causes, in the antique science of Rhabdomancy, or divination and enchantment by wands. The staff or wand of which you tell me, was, you say, made of iron or steel, and tipped with crystal. Possibly iron and crystal do really contain some properties, not hitherto scientifically analyzed, and only, indeed, potential over exceptional temperaments, which may account for the fact that iron and crystal have been favourites with all professed mystics, ancient and modern. The Delphic Pythoness had her iron tripod, Mesmer his iron bed; and many persons, indisputably honest, cannot gaze long upon a ball of crystal, but what they begin to see visions. I suspect that a philosophical cause for such seemingly preternatural effects of crystal and iron will be found in connexion with the extreme impressionability to changes in temperature, which is the characteristic both of crystal and iron. But if these materials do contain certain powers over exceptional constitutions, we do not arrive at a supernatural, but at a natural phenomenon."

---

* I may add that Dr. Kerner instances the effect of laurel-berries on the Seeress of Prevorst corresponding with that asserted by Julius Faber in the text.

† See for these unguents the work of M. Maury La Magie et l'Astrologie, &c., p. 417.

The following article, on the same subject, is from the pen of Professor Buchanan, and has recently appeared in the *Herald of Progress*. It contains the most philosophical explanation yet given of a wonderful fact, long observed, but to which little scientific attention has hitherto been given :—

WATER WITCHERY EXPLAINED.

"One of the most remarkable facts which have been neglected by the scientific, is that which has been expressed by the term Bletonism, or Water Witchery. The familiar practice in Europe and America of determining the proper location for a well, and the probable depth at which a stream of water will be found, has not received the proper attention of scientific men.

"When we examine the process by which the discovery is made we do not observe anything very rational or scientific. The water finder proceeds over the ground, holding in his hand a forked twig of witch hazel, peach, or some appropriate tree, which it is believed will turn down with considerable force and point toward the subterranean stream, whenever he stands directly over it. Such is the general opinion of water finders ; and some of them even declare that the twig turns down with sufficient force to twist it in their hands, breaking the bark. It is also believed that by holding a switch or rod in the hand by the smaller end, leaving it in a position free to move, it will adapt its direction to the course of a subterranean stream, and thus become a guide by which the stream may be traced. It is believed that on the water finder holding a small rod or twig in his hand above the site of the subterranean stream, it will soon be thrown into motion by a mysterious attraction, and begin to vibrate vertically to and from the water.

"In these opinions, although they may appear ridiculous to the man of science, we observe the form in which a familiar fact presents itself and is received by the unscientific mind. As to any attraction between the twigs and the subterranean stream of water, when no human being interferes, we have not the slightest evidence of its existence. The whole cause, therefore, of the facts and phenomena, must be found in the constitution, capacities, and pecularities of the individuals who make the experiment. The forked twig or divining rod is held in such a manner, compressed by the hand, as to be very liable, if the pressure is not carefully made, to be thrown down by the force used. Hence its turning down, even with apparent violence, is not at all surprising. But the water finder tells us, sincerely. no doubt, that he makes no effort to cause the twig to turn down, on the contrary, wishes to prevent it. Nevertheless, we know that the twig can be maintained in its erect position only by the judiciously balanced force

ADDENDA. 83

which he applies to it, and that whenever, from any cause, his force is improperly applied, it must descend, whether he wills such a result or not.

" So in the case of following the guidance of an elastic switch, it is very easy, when it is held almost balanced from one extremity swinging to and fro in an elastic manner, to change its direction by the unconscious movement of the hand of the holder; it is obvious that a very slight movement, however communicated, even the slight movements which are always experienced from the impulse of the heart, and from the movements of respiration, will be sufficient to produce a gentle vibration of the twig. By these means we can explain the movements of the divining rod of the water finder, as being entirely caused by the action of his own muscular system, independent of any anticipation on his part, or any design to produce such results.

"This reasoning, however, does not explain the wonderful fact which has been verified in thousands of instances, that the true situation of subterranean streams may be thus pointed out, and even the depth at which the water lies correctly indicated. To explain this fact we must refer to the wonderful powers of the nervous system, which recognize the influence of a medicine enveloped in a paper, or hermetically sealed in a bottle. The powers by which we recognize the influence of a medicine through solid media—by which we recognize the mental influence belonging to the contents of an unopened letter, and by which we recognize the pathological properties—are powers of a similar character to that which is concerned in water finding. It is a consequence of an impressible nervous system, that all substances around us, and at various distances, are capable of exerting an influence upon us. Sensitive persons may be powerfully affected by a magnet at fifteen or twenty feet distance. That so simple and harmless a fluid as water should exert a distinct influence upon the human constitution, at a considerable distance, is not incredible when we have witnessed parallel facts as to the operation of other agents.

" In order to explain the mysteries of Bletonism, I have selected persons of a high impressibility, with a view of determining, by the excitement of their organs, in what portion of the brain the power of the Bletonist could be located. Knowing that it was a perceptive power, I discovered that any highly impressible persons might be endued with the power of the Bletonist, by exciting sufficiently the sensitive and perceptive organs. In the greater number of highly impressible persons these organs are spontaneously sufficiently active for our purpose, and such persons are capable of becoming water finders if they exercise their power.

" I discovered, in my first examination of the subject, that any impressible person might be sensibly affected by proximity to a body of water, and that, by exciting his intuitive perceptive organs, he would be able to recognise its presence whenever he approached it. Thus, by placing a large bowl or pitcher of water upon the table, and causing the individual to pass around the room with his eyes closed, holding his hand extended horizontally, I observed that whenever his hand passed over the bowl of water, not knowing where it was, it would slightly descend as though attracted towards it. After a little experience he would he enabled, by passing his hand around the room, to recognise the spot at which he experienced the action of the water. Thus, if a bowl of water should be placed under a chair, he would be able, by placing his hand, with his eyes closed, upon each chair, to distinguish the one beneath which the water was situated. After placing his hand over a bowl of water several times, and observing a descent of his hand at each passage, it was observed that if he stood still, holding his hand in the same position, it would gradually be attracted towards the water, and descend, as if compelled by an increasing force, the muscles of the arm appearing to undergo a peculiar contractile and benumbing influence.

"Having observed these facts, I sought an opportunity to apply the principle to the case of a somewhat noted water finder. The old gentleman was brought to my office. I gave him a hint of my views as to his peculiar powers, which he received with considerable scepticism. Nevertheless, I proposed to test the water experiment, and to show him that the whole mystery of water finding consisted not in any peculiar virtue in the divining rod, but in a peculiar influence exerted by water over the human system. By the experiment of holding his arm extended in different parts of the room over a bucket of water and elsewhere, I endeavoured to convince him of the truth of the principle. He found that whenever his arm was held over the water, it was strongly disposed to descend; yet, it was not till repeated trials, in other portions of the apartment, that he could be convinced that the water exerted any peculiar influence, although his arm did not exhibit the same disposition to descend in other places. Finally, however, resolved that he would not be convinced if he could help it, he determined to hold his arm above a bucket of water, and not allow any influence from that source to effect it. He accordingly held out his hand, and steadily resisted the influence, which, nevertheless, was visibly operating and causing its descent. He continued this struggle until his arm was spasmodically agitated by his effort, and yielded the point only when he found himself unable to resist any longer.

"After giving him this demonstration of irrepressibility, I informed him that the same principles were applicable to other in fuences as well as that of water, and placed upon his forehead, in succession, the letters of Judge S., General Jackson, Mr. Calhoun, &c., from each of which he derived a striking and characteristic impression corresponding to the characters of the writers and the mode in which he was accustomed to regard them. Thus we learn that the phenomena of Bletonism are nothing more than a popular and universal mode of displaying the impressibility of the nervous system, which Neurology has demonstrated. The rod or twig, or any other apparatus for the exercise of this power, is a convenient method for its exhibition, as the muscles of the operator, while holding the twig, are affected by the influence of of the subterranean stream. But in truth, no such apparatus is necessary. The impressible Bletonist may go forth with his hand alone—may recognize subterranean streams, indicate their course and depth; and I believe may not only indicate the course of the subterranean streams, but may also determine the position of mineral strata."

An interesting account is given by our own Dr. Mayo of some experiments made by him in Germany, as follows:

"In the spring of 1847, being then at Weilbach, in Nassau, a region teeming with underground sources of water, I requested the son of the proprietor of the bathing establishment—a tall, thin, pale, white-haired youth, by name Edward Seebold—to walk in my presence up and down a promising spot of ground, holding a divining fork of hazel, with the accessories recommended M. de Tristran to beginners—that is to say, he held in his right hand three pieces of silver, besides one handle of the rod, while the handle which he held in his left hand was covered with thin silk. The lad had not made five steps, when the point of the divining fork began to ascend. He laughed with astonishment at the event, which was totally unexpected by him; and he said that he experienced a tickling or thrilling sensation in his hands. He continued to walk up and down before me. The fork had soon described a complete circle; then it described another; and so it continued to do as long as he walked thus, and as often as, after stopping, he resumed his walk. The experiment was repeated by him in my presence, with like success, several times during the ensuing month. Then the lad fell into ill health, and I rarely saw him.* However, one day I sent for him, and begged him to do me the favour of making another trial with the divining fork. He did so, but the instrument moved slowly and sluggishly; and when, having completed a semicircle, it pointed backwards towards the pit of his stomach, it stopped, and would go no farther. At the

---

* Overtaxed his powers.

same time the lad said he felt an uneasy sensation, which quickly increased to pain, at the pit of the stomach, and he became alarmed, when I bade him quit hold of one handle of the divining rod, and the pain ceased. Ten minutes afterwards I induced him to make another trial; the results were the same. A few days later, when the lad seemed still more out of health, I induced him to repeat the experiment. Now, however, the divining fork would not move at all.* I entertain little doubt that the above performances of Edward Seebold were genuine. I thought the same of the performances of three English gentlemen, and of a German, in whose hands, however, the divining rod never moved through an entire circle. In the hands of one of them its motion was retrograde, or abnormal; that is to say, it began by descending. But I met with other cases, which were less satisfactory, though not uninstructive. I should observe that, in the hands of several who tried to use it in my presence, the divining fork would not move an inch. But there were two younger brothers of Edward Seebold, and a bathmaid, and my own man, in whose hands the rod played new pranks. When these parties walked *forwards*, the instrument ascended, or moved normally; but when, by my desire, they walked *backwards*, the instrument immediately went the other way. I should observe that in the hands of Edward Seebold, the instrument moved in the same direction whether he walked forwards or backwards; and I have mentioned that at first it described in his hands a complete circle. But with the four parties I have just been speaking of, the motion of the fork was always limited in extent. When it moved normally at starting, it stopped after describing an arc of about 225°; in the same way when it moved abnormally at starting, it would stop after describing an arc of about 135°; that is to say, there was one spot the same for the two cases, beyond which it could not get. Then I found that, in the hands of my man, the divining rod would move even when he was standing still, although with a less lively action; still it stopped as before nearly at the same point. Sometimes it ascended, sometimes descended. Then I tried some experiments, touching the point with a magetic needle. I found, in the course of them, that when my man knew which way I expected the fork to move, it invariably answered my expectation; but when I had the man blindfolded the results were uncertain and contradictory. The end of all this was, that I became certain that several of those in whose hands the divining rod moves, set it in motion and directed its motion by the pressure of their fingers, and by carrying their hands nearer

---

* See my remarks and caution on the matter.

to, or father apart. In walking forward, the hands are unconsciously borne towards each other; in walking backwards, the reverse is the case. Therefore, I recommend no one to prosecute these experiments unless he can execute them himself, and unless the divining describes a complete circle in his hands; and even then he should be on his guard against self deception."

In that most interesting work, *The Autobiograpy of Heinrich Zschokke*,* the celebrated author bears his personal testimony to the power of discovering metals and fossils as well as subterranean waters in the following sentence:

"My connexion with mining operations brought me the aquaintance of many persons with whom I was much interested. The operations themselves were unimportant, for the interior of the Jura is mostly poor in metals, but an alabaster quarry which I discovered brought me into a friendly correspondence with the venerable Prince Primate, Karl von Dalberg, an I my search after salt and coal to the acqaintance of a young Rhabdomantin of twenty years old, who was sent to me by the well-known geologist, Dr. Ebel, of Zurich. In almost every canton of Switzerland are found persons endowed with the mysterious natural gift of discovering, by a peculiar sensation, the existence of subterranean waters, metals, or fossils. I have known many of them, and often put their marvellous talent to the proof. One of these was the Abbot of the Convent of St. Urban in the canton of Lucerne, a man of learning and science; and another a young woman who excelled all I have ever known. I carried her and her companion with me through several districts entirely unknown to her, but with the geological formation of which, and the position of its salt and sweet waters. I was quite familiar, and I never once found her deceived. The results of the most careful observation have compelled me at length to renounce the obstinate suspicion and incredulity I at first felt on this subject, and have presented me with a new phase of nature, although one still involved in enigmatical obscurity. To detail circumstantially every experiment I made, to satisfy myself on the point, would take up too much space at present, but I think it right to mention some of the causes which led me occasionally to vary from others in my views of Nature and of God."

Another branch of this subject is mentioned in the following passage, which we find quoted in Mr. Howitt's translation of *Ennemoser:*

"Rhabdomancy was an ancient method of divination performed by means of rods or staves. St. Jerome mentions this kind of divination in his commentary on Hosea, chap. vi. 12, where the

---

* Chapman and Hall, 1845, page 143.

prophet says, in the name of God, *My people ask counsel at their stocks; and their staff declareth unto them:* which passage that father understands of the Grecian *Rhabdomancy.* The same is met with again in Ezekiel, xxi. 21, 22, where the prophet says, *For the king of Babylon stood at the parting of the way,* at the head of the two ways, to use divination : he made his arrows bright ; or, as St. Jerome renders it, *he mixed his arrows ; he consulted with images; he looked in the liver.* If it be the same kind of divination that is alluded to in these two passages, *Rhabdomancy* must be the same kind of superstition with Belomancy : these two, in fact, are generally confounded. So much, however, is certain, that the instruments of divination mentioned by Hosea are different from those of Ezekiel : though it is possible they might use rods or arrows indifferently ; or the military men might use arrows, and the rest rods. By the laws of the Frisones it appears that the ancient inhabitants of Germany practised Rhabdomancy. The Scythians were likewise acquainted with the use of it ; and Herodotus observes (lib. vi.) that the women among the Alani sought and gathered together fine straight wands or rods, and used them for the same superstitious purposes. All these kinds of divination have been condemned by the fathers of the Church and Councils, as supposing some compact with the devil. Fludd has written several treatises on divinatiom and its different species; and Cicero has two books on the divination of the ancients, in which he confutes the whole system. Cardan also, in his 4th book, De Sapientia, describes every species of them."

There are several other very interesting facts which we wish to bring together on this subject, especially one from the pen of the late Lady Byron, who had herself this curious faculty of using the wand. We shall, therefore, resume the subject in the next number.

DIVINING RODS AND HAZEL WANDS.
Spiritual Magazine, April, 1862.

We continue this interesting subject from our last number, in which we mentioned the late Lady Byron as being possessed of the faculty. It was not Lady Byron, but Lady Milbanke, whose letter we find in Dr. Ashburner's edition of *Reichenbach*, in one of those valuable notes with which the Doctor has enriched his translation of that work. We cannot mention these notes without strongly recommending them to our readers as containing information from one of the most philosophical and scientific minds we have amongst us. On this subject, on which we are now bringing together a few facts, we find an elaborate and luminous essay, in the shape of a note, and containing the letter of Milbanke, which we have somewhat abbreviated and condensed into what follows. Dr. Ashburner says that in the counties of Somerset, Devon, and Cornwall, the facts on this subject are well known, and the practice of dowsing, as it is called, has been cultivated time out of mind. In France the men of scientific pursuits have for the most part ridiculed the use of the baguette, notwithstanding abundant evidence in various parts of the country being extant of the success which had attended the practice of the sourciers. The Baron von Reichenbach has established facts regarding the emanations of light from graves, which are quite as remarkable as the proofs of emanations taking place from metals or from running water. Now that the Baron's researches, and the concurrent testimony of the cultivators of mesmeric science, have established that certain individuals are more susceptible of magnetic impressions than others, it will not be pronounced *impossible* that subterraneous running water may influence some persons, and not others. In different classes of animals the sensitive powers are known to vary greatly, as they do among those of the same species.

The following extracts will further illustrate the subject :—

"Although the effects or motion of the divining rod, when in the proximity of springs, has been and is to this day considered by most philosophers a mere illusion, yet I think the following brief observations relating to this subject, and which were communicated to Dr. Hutton by a lady of rank, with the account of her subsequent experiments performed before him, his family, and a number of friends (as given in the doctor's translation of Montucla's edition of Ozanam's Recreations), must convince the most incredulous that in the hands of some persons, in certain situations, the baguette is forcibly acted upon by some hitherto unknown invisible cause. This evidence was brought about in the following manner. Soon after the publication of the former edition of the Recreations, the editor received by the post the following well-written pseudonymous letter on the subject of this problem. The letter in question is dated Feb. 10, 1805, and, as with the whole of the correspondence it would be too long for our limits, I shall select such parts only as are immediately essential to a right understanding of the subject.

"The lady observes, 'In the year 1772 (I was then nineteen) I passed six months at Aix, in Provence. I there heard the popular story of one of the fountains in that city having been discovered some generations before, by a boy who always expressed an aversion from passing one particular spot, crying out *there was water*. This was held by myself, and the family I was with, in utter contempt. In the course of the Spring, the family went to pass a week at the Chateau d'Ansonis, situated a few miles to the north of the Durance, a tract of country very mountainous, and where water was very ill supplied. We found the Marquis d'Ansonis busied in erecting what might be termed a miniature aqueduct, to convey a spring the distance of half a league, or nearly as much, to his chateau, which spring he asserted had been found out by a peasant, who made the discovery of water his occupation in that country, and maintained himself by it, and was known by the appellation of *l' Homme à la Baguette*. This account was received with unbelief, almost amounting to derision. The Marquis, piqued at being discredited, sent for the man, and requested we would witness the experiment. A large party of French and English accordingly attended. The man was quite a peasant in manners and appearance: he produced some twigs cut from a hazel, of different sizes and strength, only they were forked branches, and hazel was preferred, as forking more equally than most other trees; but it is not requisite that the angle should be of any particular number of degrees. He held the ends of the twigs between each fore finger and thumb, with the vertex pointing downwards. Standing where there was no water, the baguette remained motionless; walking gradually to the spot where the spring was *underground*, the twig was sensibly affected; and as he approached the spot, began to *turn round*; that is, the vortex raised itself, and turned towards his body, and continued to turn until the point was vertical; it then again descended outwards, and continued to turn, describing a circle as long as he remained standing over the spring, or till one or both branches were broken by the twisting, the ends being firmly grasped by the fingers and thumbs, and the hands kept stationary, so that the rotary motion must of course twist them. After seeing him do this repeatedly, the whole party tried the baguette in succession, but without effect. I chanced to be the last. No sooner did I hold the twig as directed, than it began to move as with him, which startled me so much that I dropped it, and felt considerably agitated. I was, however, induced to resume the experiment, and found the effect perfect. I was then told it was no very unusual thing, many having that faculty, which, from what has since come to my knowledge, I have reason to believe is true. On my return to England I forbore to let this faculty (or whatever you may term it) be known, fearing to become the topic of conversation or discussion. But two years afterwards, being on a visit to a nobleman's house, Kimbolton, Huntingdonshire, and his lady lamenting that she was disappointed of building a dairy-house in a spot she particularly wished, because there was *no water* to be found—a supply she looked on as essential—under *promise of secrecy* I told her I would endeavour to find a spring. I accordingly procured some hazel twigs, and in the presence of herself and husband, walked over the ground proposed, till the twig turned with *considerable force*. A stake was immediately driven into the ground to mark the spot, which was not very distant from where they had before sunk. They then took me to another and distant building in the park, and desired me to try there: I found the baguette turn *very strongly*, so that it soon twisted and broke: the gentleman persisted that there was no water there, unless at a great depth, the foundation being very deep (a considerable stone cellar), and that no water appeared when they dug for it. I could only reply that I knew no more than from the baguette turning, and that I had too little experience of its powers or certainty to answer for the truth of its indication. He then acknowledged that when the building was erected they were obliged to drive piles for the whole foundation, as they met with nothing but a quicksand. This induced him to dig in the spot I first directed; they met with a very fluent spring; the dairy was built, and it is at this time supplied by it.

"'I could give a long detail of other trials I have made, all of which have been convincing of the truth, but they would be tedious. For some years past I have been indifferent about its becoming known, and have consequently been frequently requested to show the experiment, which has often been done to persons of high estimation for understanding and knowledge, and I believe they have *all been convinced*. Three people I have met with, who have, on trying, found themselves possessed of the same faculty. I shall only add one more particular incident. Having once shown it to a party, we returned into the house to a room on the ground floor; I was again asked *how I held the rod*; taking one in my hand I found it turned immediately; on which an old lady, mother to the gentleman of the house, said *that room* was formed out of an old cloister, in which cloister was a *well*, simply boarded over when they made the room.

"'L'Homme à la Baguette, from experience, could with tolerable accuracy tell the depth at which the springs were, and their volume from the force with which the baguette turns; I can only give a rough guess. In strong *frost* I think its powers not so great; on a bridge or in a boat it has *no effect*, the water must be *underground* to affect the baguette, and running through wooden pipes acts the same as a spring. I can neither make the baguette turn where there is *no water*, nor prevent it from turning where there is any, and I am perfectly ignorant *of the cause why it turns*. The only sensation I am conscious of is an emotion similar to that felt on being startled by sudden noise, or surprise of any kind. I generally use a baguette about six inches from the vertex to the end of the twigs where they are cut off. I shall most probably be in London next winter, and will (if you wish it) afford you an opportunity of making your own observations on this curious fact."

The lady having arrived in London, wrote to Dr. Hutton to inform him that she proposed being at Woolwich on Friday, the 30th inst. (May, 1806) at eleven in the forenoon.

"Accordingly," says Dr. H., "At the time appointed, the lady with all her family arrived at my house on Woolwich Common, where, after preparing the rods, &c., they walked out to the grounds, accompanied by the individuals of my own family and some friends, when Lady ——— showed the experiment several times in different places, holding the rods, &c., in the manner as described in her ladyship's first letter above given. In the places where I had good reason to know that no water was to be found, the rod was always quiescient; but in other places, where I knew there was water below the surface, the rods turned slowly and regularly, in the manner above described, till the twigs twisted themselves off below her fingers, which were considerably indented by so forcibly holding the rods between them. All the company present stood close round the lady, with all eyes intently fixed on her hands and the rods, to watch if any particular motion might be made by the fingers—but in vain; nothing of the kind was perceived, and all the company could observe no cause or reason why the rod should move in the manner as they were seen to do."

There can be no impropriety in stating now that the lady in question was the Honourable Lady Milbanke, wife of Sir Ralph Milbanke, Bart. (afterwards Noel) and mother of the late Dowager Lady Byron, the wife and widow of the great poet. A very interesting analagous statement relating to the same person will be found in the *Quarterly Review* for March, 1820 : No. xliv. vol. 22.

Lately in France, the Count de Tristan has published a work on the subject, which I have been unable to procure; but I have a most interesting volume containing two memoirs by M. Thouvenel, a physician of reputation in France, who was commissioned, in the year 1781, to the king, to analyse and report upon the mineral and medicinal waters of the kingdom. The author undertakes a patient and laborious investigation in the spirit of a philosopher, and regards his inquiries as leading to a new thread in the tangled skein of physics, which, like any single fact of science, may lead to the discovery of a thousand others. Thouvenel found a man named Bléton, whose business was that

ADDENDA. 93

of a discoverer of springs by means of a divining rod; and upon this man he made more than 600 observations, many of them in the presence of more than 150 persons, mostly of important station, and very credible from their high character, who testify to the truth of the observed phenomena. Among others was M. Jadalet, Professor of Physic at Nancy, a man eminent for his abilities, who was not only a witness of these experiments, but was actually concerned in the greatest part of them. As in the case of Lady Milbanke, with Bléton, an *internal feeling* was coincident with the movement of the rod. Whenever this man was in a place where there existed subterraneous waters, he was immediately sensible of a lively impression, referable to the diaphragm, which he called his "*commotion.*" This was followed by a sense of oppression in the upper part of the chest; at the same time he felt a shock, with general tremor and chilliness, staggering of the legs, stiffness of the wrists with twitchings, a concentrated pulse, which gradually diminished. All these symptoms were more or less strong according to the volume and depth of the water, and they were more sensibly felt when Bléton *went in a direction against* the subterranean current, than where he followed *its course.* Stagnant water underground did not affect him; nor did open sheets of water, ponds, lakes, or rivers affect him. The nervous system of this man must have been susceptible, since he was more sensibly affected by change of weather and variations in the state of the atmosphere than other persons: otherwise he appeared healthy. A severe acute disorder had absolutely at one time deprived him of the faculty of perceiving water, and his sensibility in this respect did not return until three months after his recovery; so that if he were sensitive, he could not be classed among the sick *sensitive*s. But however remarkable these constitutional peculiarities may have been, there was in Bléton's case a more than usual distinctness in the behaviour of the divining rod.

It was found that whether the trials were made in this manner or over masses of coal, subterraneous currents of water, or metallic veins, the divining rod indicated a determined sphere of electric activity, and was in fact an electrometrical rod. "Of all the phenomena relating to the distinctions of fossil bodies," says Thouvenel, "acting by their electric emanations, doubtless the most surprising is this; upon the mines of iron, of whatever kind they may be, the rods supported by the fingers of Bléton turned constantly upon their axis, from behind forward, as upon the mines of coal; while upon other metallic veins, as upon other metals extracted from their mines, the rotary movement took place in the contrary direction, that is to say, from before backwards. This particular movement, which never varies while

Bléton is in a perpendicular position over mines or upon metals, presents revolutions as rapid and as regular as the revolutions in the contrary direction upon the mines of iron and of coal."

Dr. Ashburner adds as follows:—

A highly susceptible girl, the lady's maid of a very clever and intelligent friend of mine, residing in Hertfordshire, offers, when she is mesmerised, a great many deeply interesting phenomena. I have repeatedly mentioned her as Harriet P———. She is as guileless and as good a being as can be met with, and is much beloved by her excellent and amiable mistress, who has repeatedly addressed me on her case. If a piece of hazel stick or whitethorn be presented to Harriet, she grasps it and sleeps mesmerically in less than a minute. The sleep is at first very intense and deep, and then the stick is held so firmly that the spasmodic state of the muscles renders it very difficult for even a powerful bystander to turn it in her hand. Mary Anne Douglas and several others of my patients have exhibited the same phenomena. In two of the cases a very curious point has been remarked. If the hazel or whitethorn stick be held with the pointed end upwards, that end which is upwards when it grows from the ground, the force of attraction is so energetic that these individuals cannot resist their inclination to grasp it with both hands. One of them will rush towards it from a considerable distance, and will with extreme eagerness run from the bottom to the top of the house in order to have the pleasure of grasping it. If she succeed in getting hold of it before its direction is reversed, her delight is unbounded; she becomes intoxicated, and soon passes into a state of deep unconscious sleep. If, however, the stick be turned rapidly with its pointed end downwards, a repulsive force operates, and each patient feels a repugnance to it. If the stick be allowed to be held in both hands, and a piece of gold, or of platinum, or of cobalt, or of nickel, or the pointed end of a rock crystal be held to it, in each experiment there is a burning sensation complained of, and an endeavour is made to loosen the hold on the stick, with ludicrous haste. A gentleman who had been often put into mesmeric sleep, remarked, on holding successively several pieces of these sticks, that a sensation of heat was communicated to his hand in each instance, and he felt a strong tendency to sleep. Susan L., a highly susceptible person, exclaimed, while in a sleep-waking state, "that a shower of fine small sparks of fire," came from a piece of hazel which happened to be in my hand. She did not see this from ash or from fir, but invariably saw it from every piece of hazel or from whitethorn that was brought near her. On numerous occasions experiments were made to test the accuracy of her

repetitions on observing these things, and she invariably gave the same answers to the questions on the same subjects. Subsequently, eight other individuals were separately examined as to their susceptibilities to different kinds of wood. Each gave the same results and saw the sparks of fire. In many other cases, the impressionability being different, the hazel and white-thorn had no perceptible effects; the patients handling the bits of stick without observing heat or sparks, and failing to grasp them spasmodically. But Harriet P———r's impressionability was put to a very useful purpose. Her mistress had heard of the practice of dowsing for water, and in a letter to a correspondent, now before me, writes thus under date of July, 1845 :—
"We made a curious experiment here sometime since with Harriet P———. We have very bad water here, and have long been unable to find a good spring. Mr. G. has in vain dug and dug and dug for one. I proposed the divining rod, for, said I, Dr. Ashburner would not think it a foolish experiment. Harriet P——— was willing, so we went forth to a field the most likely one for a spring; Mr. and Mrs. G., myself, and two friends staying here. We put Harriet to sleep by the hazel stick, she grasped it so tightly that we were obliged to use the gold chain; she then held it only in one hand, and immediately began to walk, taking her own way. She went very carefully for about 20 yards, then suddenly stopped as if she had been shot. Not a word was uttered by any one. We all looked on, and were not a little surprised to see the rod slowly turn round until her hand was almost twisted backwards. It looked as if it must pain her. Still no one spoke. Suddenly she exclaimed, 'There! there! don't you see the stick turn? the water is here —under my hand, I see, oh I see—let me look—don't speak to me—I like to look.' 'How deep is the water?' said Mrs. G., speaking to Harriet's fingers. 'Oh, about three feet, I can't quite tell, but it is here.' In a moment, to our astonishment, she sunk down on the grass, took the stick again in both her hands, and seemed to like it as if it could feel. We made a strange group round her, as we were all much astonished to see what we had come there to see, but still it astonished us, she seemed so like a little witch. We marked the place, and after a few minutes we awoke her. In the evening she was again mesmerised to sleep, and we asked her what she saw at the spring. 'Why I saw water—water everywhere.' 'Then,' said I, 'how do you know where the spring is?' 'Oh, because it goes trinkle, trinkle—I know it is there.' 'Why did you sit down?' 'Why, because I was so giddy; it seemed as if all was water but the little piece of ground I stood upon ;—oh, I saw so much water, all fresh, but no sea; I tried to see the sea,

but I could not—I could not at all.' Mr. G. caused a large hole to be dug at the place, and just at the depth of three feet the water was found. A brick well has been constructed, and there is a good supply of excellent water. No one could doubt of the action of the rod, it turned so evidently *of itself* in her hand. Of course when awake Harriet knew nothing of the circumstance."

So many and so various are the testimonies and facts relating to the divining rod, that it would be tedious to recite the hundreds of respectable documents offered by those authors who have written on this subject. Lately a work, by Tardy de Montravel, printed in 1871, entitled *Mémoire Physique et Medicinal sur la Baguette Divinatoire*, has fallen into my hands, and it abounds in testimonies as to the truth of the same class of facts. One of the most curious works I have seen on the subject is a little book with the title of *La Physique occulte, ou Traité de la Baguette Divinatoire et de son Utilité pour la découverte des sources d'eaux, des mineres, des trésors cachez, des voleurs, et des meurtriers fugitifs, avec des principes qui expliquent les phenomenès les plus obscurs de la Nature*, par M. L. L. de Vallemont, Ph.D, et Ph., &c. This work, embellished with plates illustrating the different kinds of divining rods, with the various modes of holding them for use, appeared at the latter part of the seventeenth century, and passed through several editions in France as well as in Holland. It is remarkable for much curious literary and historical learning, and for able statements of the arguments which were used in the controversies, rife at that period, on the realities of the facts under consideration. It contains a curious catalogue of a great number of mines discovered in France, by means of the divining rod, made out by a German mineralogist employed for the purpose by Cardinal de Richelieu. But the most singular part of the book is the powerfully authenticated history of Jacques Aymar, a peasant, who, constitutionally impressionable, guided by the divining rod, followed a murderer for more than 45 leagues on land, and more than 30 leagues by sea, and, I may add, found him.

THE DIVINING ROD IN AUSTRALIA.
Spiritual Magazine, August, 1867.

In the area of Kiora, lying to the southward of Ararat, the settlers who are very anxious to discover springs of water upon their selections, have engaged the services of an old man, apparently between sixty and seventy years of age, who professes to discover springs by the aid of a divining-rod. He has already pointed out spots where he confidently states water will be found at a moderate depth, and the farmers are now engaged in practically proving his skill. We are told the diviner holds a slender strip of steel between the finger and thumb of both hands, and walks about the land with it in this position. When water is approached, the rod trembles violently, and the motion ceases as the place is left. One of the settlers, Mr. Tomkins, with the view of testing his accuracy, had the diviner blindfolded (after pointing out the spot where the water would be found) and taken to another portion of his land, but he states that the motion of the rod led him, with but little hesitation, back to the same place. The old man refuses to take money for his services till water be obtained, and when proved to exist asks £3 from each individual. He states that the rod was owned by his father, and that it will not indicate water in the hands of any of his brothers. While engaged at Kiora he showed some of the farmers letters which he had received from a number of squatters engaging his services on their stations in a similar capacity; and he left to fulfil these engagements, with a view of returning for payment when the sinking is concluded. He professes to name within three feet of the depth at which water will be obtained, but cannot say if it will prove fresh or salt.—*Melbourne Argus*, February 25th, 1867.

DIVINERS.

Spiritual Magazine, June, 1868.

A good deal of attention was paid by the newspapers to certain alleged achievements of two diviners, or dowsers, about twenty years ago. They were West of England men named Adams and Mapstone. A farmer, near Wedmore, in Somerset, wishing for a supply of water on his farm, applied to Mapstone. Mapstone used a hazel rod in the usual way, and when he came over a particular spot, declared that water would be found 15 or 20 feet beneath the surface. Digging was, therefore, commenced at that spot, and water appeared at a depth of 19 feet. The other expert, Adams, who claimed to have been instrumental in the discovery of nearly a hundred springs in the West of England, went, one day, by invitation, to the house of Mr. Phippen, a surgeon, at Wedmore, to dowse for water. He walked about in the garden behind Mr. Phippen's house, until the stick became so agitated that he could not keep it steady; it bent down at a spot which, he asserted, must have water underneath it. Mr. Phippen caused a digging to be made, and water was really found at the spot indicated. As a means of testing Adams's powers in relation to metals, three hats were placed in a row in the kitchen, and three silver spoons under one of the hats. Adams walked among the hats, and his rod told him which of them covered the treasure. Then three kinds of valuables—gold, silver, and jewels—were placed under three hats, one kind under each, and he found out which was which. On another occasion he dowsed for water in the grounds of the Rev. Mr. Foster, of Sedbury, in Gloucestershire. Using the same method as before, he announced the presence of water at a particular spot, 20 feet beneath the surface. A pamphlet, published by Mr. Phippen, concerning these curious facts, attracted the attention of Mr. Marshall, partner in the great flax factory, at Leeds. Water was wanted at the mill, and the owners were willing to see whether dowsing could affect anything in the matter. Mr. Marshall invited Adams to come down and search for springs. On one occasion, when blindfolded, Adams failed, but hit the mark pretty nearly in the second attempt, excusing himself for the first failure, on the ground that "he was not used to be blindfolded." Of the main experiments, Mr. Marshall afterwards said, in a letter to the newspapers, "I tested Adams by taking him over some deep borings at our manufactory, where he could have no possible guide from anything he could see ; and he certainly pointed out nearly the position of the springs, as shown by the produce of the bore holes, some being much more productive than others. The same was the result at another factory, where Adams could have had no guide from what he saw, and could not have got information otherwise."—"*Stick* (*not Table*) *Turning*," in *All the Year Round*.

DIVINING ROD.
Spiritual Magazine, May, 1868.

A writer in the *Gentleman's Magazine* asserts the virtues of these rods, and gives figures of them, and directions for their use, vol. xxi., p. 507. Soon after, another writer gave a very striking instance of the reality of the power of such rods. He states that Linnæus, on a journey to Scania, hearing the virtues of the divining rod highly extolled, determined to try it. He hid a purse of one hundred ducats under a ranunculus, which grew by itself in a meadow, and bade his secretary, the operator with the wand, find it, if he could. The ranunculus was speedily trodden down by the throng of people, and, for some time, the rod discovered nothing. Linnæus then attempted to find the purse, but could not, and persisted in seeking for it in a particular quarter. The Secretary having tried that quarter, declared that it was not there, and eventually, following his rod, found the purse in a different direction. Linnæus adds, that another such an experiment would have made a proselyte of him.*

I think, however, that I have given sufficient proofs (possibly I may have wearied you with them). My only object in giving any is that you may compare the statements of M. Baritel with subsequent writers, and with this apology conclude this chapter; the next will relate my own experiences and experiments in discovering mines, minerals, &c., extending over a period of 25 years, constituting an entirely new discovery, and one by which the rod may be dispensed with. May I ask the favour to overlook my brusquerie and deficient construction of the English language, as I am but a workman.

CHAPTER II.

For a clear understanding of this chapter it will be well if you are conversant with the arts of Mesmerism, and so called Electro Biology. These two terms I use as by them the public are better acquainted with the phenonema, premising, however, that Mesmerism, Animal Magnetism, and the Odic force, are three names for one and the same electrical force, emanating from all persons, and that Electro Biology and Electro Psychology are identical. So for the sake of not being misunderstood (though I dislike the terms), I will use

---

* The reason of the difficulty of finding the purse will be explained in the chapter devoted to my own experiences.

the words Mesmerism and Biology when requisite, and also point out the difference of the two states, which, though produced by the same will-force, are not identical but distinct, for Mesmerism, or the visible result it produces, is the effect of sympathy with the person mesmerised or magnetised, whereas Biology is the science of impressions received *by* the person acted *on*.

In Mesmerism there must be perfect accord between the magnetiser and the person magnetised. What the magnetiser sees, feels, hears, tastes, is readily perceived by the person mesmerised, and not only so, but what the mesmeriser wills is also the will of the one mesmerised, by joint sympathy and accord, and union of will and desire between both parties. It would be foreign to my purpose to enumerate the various states this will-force produces, as there are numerous works on the subject that shew all its phases, which, for an accurate understanding of the subject, are well worth studying, were it only for the curious and extraordinary matter they contain—(these may be procured at Messrs. Heywood's, Catherine Street, Strand) —still, as I proceed, it may be necessary to refer to them, so that you may better comprehend me.

In the biological state the person psychologised has no such feeling or sympathy with the operator, he is entirely independent of him, and commonly resists with all his or her will or power, and, again, the mesmerised usually hears no voice but that of the magnetiser; in the psychological state the biolised is *en rapport* with all present. This is proof of the electrical difference between the two states. I think it here necessary to state, that comparatively few, if any, are naturally in the mesmeric or somnambulic state, but that a very large proportion of mankind are in a naturally biological state, and ready to your hand to use. Do me the favour not to forget this, as you will require it presently, but clearly understand that the same electro nervous fluid, which is at all times emanating from all, produces both states by the will of the operator, though the results may be and are different.

For the clear comprehension of the difference between these two states, it will I think be advisable that I give a copious extract from a small pamphlet published by myself, called "Fascination." This is necessary should you be inclined to carry out the experiments that are to follow in the discovery of springs, minerals, mines, &c., for the state termed "Clairvoyance" will not serve your purpose so well as the psychological or biological state; my experience teaches me that it is not so certain in its results, besides that the effects produced by the action of the hazel rod are not so readily removed, which are absolutely necessary to be done for the safety of the sensitive, or salivation will ensue. Besides that you require your sensitive always clear and in health, and it would be most selfish and ungenerous to neglect the precautions to obviate such a misfortune as the loss of it through your neglect.

With these few remarks, and with the supposition that you are unacquainted with the subject, I bring to your notice the art of Electro Psychology. It is certain that this state is induced by the action of your mind acting positively on the person operated upon, who is naturally, or who may be rendered, electro-negative to yourself. This is very simply tested in the following manner:—If before an audience, ask as many as can conveniently be accommodated on the platform, seat them, and to each give a round disc of zinc about two inches in diameter, in the centre of which is fixed a piece of copper half an inch in diameter; request them all to look intently on the copper in the centre (the disc being placed on the palm), at about a foot distant, for the space of twenty minutes, and to keep, if possible, their minds perfectly tranquil, and not look about them. At the end of that time, collect your discs, and carefully examine each person; those whose eyes are wide open reject, but those whose eyes are closed, or have a tendency to close, treat separately in this manner.* Take the person's hand, and with moderate but firm pressure press on the Median nerve (this nerve is situated at the base of the thumb joint, and not easy to find, but for fear of missing it cover with your thumb the part just below the joint and pulse) for about a minute; at the same time, with moderate pressure, press (with the other hand) on the organ of individuality, situated in the

---

* Or you may, if you have a galvanic battery and coil, dispense with the zinc discs, and cause all the persons upon whom you are experimenting to join hands for about fifteen minutes, so forming a chain, and by each end person holding the wire all will receive a very slight continuous shock, which must be graduated so as not to cause inconvenience to them, but just so as to be distinctly felt. I prefer the zinc discs, having obtained better results with them.

middle of the lower part of the forehead. If the person by this act proves to be electro-negative to you, say, in a firm, resolute manner, and voice with plenty of confidence, "You cannot open your eyes," and *determine* within yourself that *he shall not*. Should he, however, succeed or partially do so, again put the fingers on the organ of individuality, and, with the disengaged hand, gently stroke downwards the eyelids, *resolving* that they *shall close;* and should you fail this time, be not discouraged, but remember that almost all persons can be brought under your influence by repeated trials, even though it may require a hundred; generally speaking, it requires two. About five per cent. are naturally subject to your influence; and if there be any among them known to be, or apparently, suffering from any ailment, you can at once afford relief, and probably cure, by the simple action of your WILL (using, of course, the manipulation before described, with the exception of the zinc discs); and at the same time it is advisable always to say to the patient, "You are well," or, "You are better," or, "To-morrow you will be cured." But in the event of the persons being in health, proceed with the *seance* by addressing them thus, "You cannot open your eyes," "I told you that you could not," "It is of no use trying," or anything else that you please like it; or say promptly "You cannot lift your leg," "You cannot move your arm," and so on.

If you are successful in controlling the movements of the body, try the emotions of the mind, in evoking joy, fear, surprise; but never rage, or you may, perchance get a thrashing for your pains, although you may possess the strength of a giant to resist the attack. If the person is then perfectly subservient to your will, mentally and bodily, you can cause him to think and do as you please—cause him to imagine himself a horse, a windmill, a steamboat, that his sex is changed—cause him to see things that exist only in your own mind—make him imagine that his head is rolling on the floor, and set him to catch it, cause him to make any absurd noise, to imitate animals, which he will do most drolly, amidst roars of laughter, in which he himself will most heartily join, probably, with a grave face, which considerably enhances the fun; and all this is accomplished without any damage to himself. Of course you will take especial care not to cause him to do anything disagreeable to himself or the company. If he stutters, or has any other bad habit, make him promise to abandon it for ever, and he will do so, provided that you exert your will conjointly with his for that purpose. When you have finished experimenting, and desire to restore him to his normal condition, tell him distinctly that you are about to do so, in whatever words you please, and, with the *will* that he shall be so restored, blow sharply on his forehead a few times. This will be certain to remove your influence from him.

I shall conclude this first part of my address with a remark to which I request you to pay particular attention. Never use this power for any bad or unworthy purpose; for all good things may be abused. It is but right also that I should put you on your guard against those who may endeavour to influence you without your consent, for I have before told you that many are naturally sensitive to others. If you suspect that any one wishes to do so, simply lay your hand for a few seconds on the forehead (in fact mesmerise yourself), and *determine* that they shall not influence or govern you in any manner whatever, and no one can possibly do so. I may here incidentally say, that the knowledge of the positions of the cerebral organs will be of great service to you in assisting you to poduce the various effects before described.

The Second Part to which I call your attention will be MESMERISM, or the science of sympathy with the patient, and which is, as I will explain, a distinct science from Electro-Biology, which is, as before stated, the science of impressions, whereby the person impressed simply obeys the will of the operator, his senses being entirely independent of himself, frequently resisting with all his force ; but in the science of Mesmerism, or Animal Magnetism, the person mesmerised is in perfect sympathy and accord with the mesmeriser, and that which he (the mesmeriser) feels, sees, smells, hears, tastes, or wills, is perceived by the mesmerisee, but who, when awakened from the mesmeric sleep, has no remembrance of that which has happened during the period he has been in that state, except when told to do so by the operator before awakening ; whereas, in the Electro-Biological state, he knows all that transpires, without the power to prevent, however ridiculous it may be. This explanation is sufficient to show that the two sciences, though analogous, are distinct ; yet both these states are induced by the same nervous fluid emanating from the operator. I will now proceed to instruct you in the practice and application of Mesmerism. In the first place, I wish you to understand that you are a living electrical machine, and that there is at all times an emanation, or force, escaping or evolving naturally from you, and that this force can be projected upon and received by a person susceptible to it, the hands, by the exercise of your *will*, acting as conductors. This force, under proper management, cures the sick, simply by imparting to the part which is deficient in the recipient more life and health. It can be directed by your will into the most remote part of the human body, and cause that part, if not too much diseased, to re-compose new healthy particles; in fact, consumption, cancer, epilepsy, and certain forms of paralysis, and other dangerous maladies (passing over minor ills), have been in hundreds of cases cured by its use alone. Although I prefer using it as an adjunct to medicine, under medical direction, I should not hesitate, did I see any one suffering, to try and relieve him—of course by permission of the sufferer; but in certain emergent cases, such as epilepsy, without it.

The method that I have used for the last twenty five years to induce sleep, is very simple. The patient being comfortably seated in an easy chair, I request him to be calm, and look steadfastly into my eyes, at the same time taking both his hands into mine in such a manner that the insides of his and my thumbs touch firmly, WILLING that he shall pass into the mesmeric sleep. If, after having done so for about ten minutes, I perceive the eyelids to be tremulous, and the eyes moist, I lay his hands quietly on his lap, and proceed to make the usual mesmeric passes slowly over the eyes, head, and shoulders, and off the tips of the fingers in this manner:—Raise the hands, palms downwards, but closed; open the hands when over the head, and bring them down as stated; close them whilst raising them again, and repeat. If this course be continued for twenty minutes, the effect is perceptible; but perhaps you may, succeed in inducing the sleep in ten minutes, to deepen which, in all cases, lay the hand lightly on the pit of the stomach and remain tranquil for a few minutes; or the sleep may be deepened by gently pressing the eyelids, or by slowly passing the hand over the head (from back to front), or by softly breathing on the patient's hands. When the sleep is induced, take *especial care*, I repeat it, *especial care*, that no person but yourself touch or in any way interfere with your patient, or even come too close to him, for by so doing the spectator, though meaning no harm, may unintentionally magnetise him and produce convulsions. This is called a case of cross mesmerism. To awaken your patient, all that you have to do is to express firmly to him, in any words you please, your wish that he shall awake; and in a minute or so make *upward* passes with that desire, until the eyes be open. If the eyes shou'd afterwards feel stiff, blow sharply on the forehead to remove the inconvenience. Remember that the breath is dual in its action; if you blow sharply it removes the mesmeric effect, but if you breath softly, and with WILL, you mesmerise most powerfully. I have, however, in my experience found that comparatively few pass into the sleep, yet I have cured them without producing it, or in any way apparently affecting them, for the simple repetition of the process causes an accumulation of the magnetism, or magnetic fluid, in the system, and with it, health. In plain words, it restores the polarity of the human body, the reversal of which is disease, call it by what name you please. And now you will do me the favour not to forget (though you may smile at it) at all times when making passes over the sick, to shake your hands either on each side of, or behind you, WILLING in your own mind to eject the sickness that you are removing. For want of this precaution, I have known mesmerists take to themselves, and retain, the diseases that they were curing. It is also well to wash your hands after you have finished with the patient.

Having shown you how to mesmerise generally, under ordinary circumstances, I think it advisable to instruct you how to do so locally, in particular cases; that is, how to concentrate your power upon, and to confine it to that part of the system which may be in pain, inflamed, or otherwise deficient of health. If the person suffers from headache, make the passes (downwards in all cases), over the forehead, temples, behind the ears, to the shoulders, down the arms, and off to the tips of the fingers. Do this for about fifteen minutes, when the pain will be relieved, but if the pain be of long standing, repeat daily until cured.

If the patient suffers from an open ulcer, make circular passes over it with the tips of the fingers of the right hand, for about ten minutes, WILLING at the same time, that you will project health on it, then think firmly, "I will gather up the disease in my hand,' and suiting the action to the thought, mentally pull it

ADDENDA.

out, and throw it from you. Continue this process daily until cure is effected.

If you have a child suffering with rickets, or that is weakly, strip it before the fire to avoid risk of cold, and lay the left hand on its head, with the right hand make firm, slow, vigorous passes by contact, down the spine, thighs, and legs, for about twenty minutes, with the fixed benevolent intention of imparting your vitality to it. Repeat night and morning, until strong.

For toothache or earache (if agreeable to the patient), lay on the part affected a piece of thin clean flannel, and breathe on it powerfully, with long expirations, for a few minutes. I never knew this method fail to relieve; generally, by repetition, it effects a cure. If your friend has an attack of the gout, go like a friend and relieve him; at all events, try to do so until the colchicum comes from the chemists; if the pain has reached the head and breast, as it not unfrequently does, make strong passes (in earnest, mind) downwards over the head, breast, thighs, and legs, and when you come to the feet let your hands remain over them for a few seconds, then in your mind gather in your hands the pain, or cause of pain, and, with a strong pull, pull it out, and be mindful to throw it from you as before prescribed. Continue this process unti your patient be relieved, and repeat if requisite. If the pain be only in the knees and feet, commence to mesmerise at the thighs. This process may also be successfully applied to rheumatism and all painful neuralgic cases. And now, as far as space will permit, a fair insight into the science and application of Mesmerism is given, but I would advise, until more thoroughly acquainted with it, no attempt to cure epilepsy or skin diseases should be made, since, on account of their peculiar nature, these maladies require experienced treatment; and, with this advice, I will add a few words on the mode of mesmerising water for the use of the sick, either to wash with for skin diseases, or to make tea and coffee, or to use as ordinary drinking water. Take a quart of water in an open jug, hold it on your knee with the left hand, and *point* and *jerk* the tips of the fingers of the right hand over the water for about twenty minutes, with the determination that you will charge it with your influence for the benefit of the patient, and *resolving* that your magnetism shall permeate the whole, and it will do so. Or, if agreeable, take a quart bottle, and insert into it a piece of tin gaspipe in the form of the letter S, breathe through it for about five minutes to the bottom of the water. This latter process is more powerful in its action on the water than the first. This magnetised water is a powerful restorative, and may be drank freely. If your patient be susceptible you may, if you please, charge the water in a dark room, and he will see the vitality proceeding from you into the water in the shape of vapour or scintillations. Like homœopathic medicines, this water must be kept in the dark.

In concluding, I earnestly beg that no use of this power which exists in every human being be attempted for a bad purpose, nor when you are not in health, nor for a trial of strength, nor to magnetise a lady unless a third person be present, but to employ it soberly and fearlessly, with a sincere and generous spirit, for the benefit and advantage of your fellow creatures, asking, in faith, for a return to men of that gift which was common amongst the early Christians, viz., the gift of healing.

It may be that you are surprised at my statement that water can be mesmerised. I have but to say that all created things can be so treated, and the power inherent to each increased marvellously (see Ashburner, Teste, Deleuze, and many others on Animal Magnetism). This leads me to say the hazel rod acts but feebly in the hands of some, but by making a few mesmeric passes down the rod its effects are increased tenfold, so that those who are sensitive to its influence but in a low degree can have it enhanced, and so rendered much more sensitive. This induced state may sometimes be necessary, but is not so with those who have the power well developed, because the superinduction would interfere with, and probably damage, their clear sensitiveness, to the normal action of the rod. The method by which it is done is very simple and as follows :—Let the mesmerist, biologist, or experimentalist, take the straight hazel rod in the left hand, and make mesmeric passes for a few minutes from the point down to the root end, observing to close the fingers each time the right is lifted to repeat the pass, so as not to demagnetise the rod, but when it is necessary to do so, reverse the rod in the left hand, and make as many passes from the root to the point. By this means the rod will again be brought to its normal state (see experiment 4, page 114).

At the time when I first became conversant with

the science of Animal Magnetism, of course I rode my hobby to death, but for all that when experience had taught me properly how to use it by its application I performed several remarkable cures, and while attending a gentleman residing at Eastbourne, in 1851, I became acquainted with a market gardener of that place, who kindly invited myself and family to his garden, giving us the free use of it. In course of conversation he stated that in consequence of there being no water on the land he rented, that he should not apply for a new lease, but leave at Michaelmas. Knowing my wife's faculty (she is lame) I sent our servant girl home for a certain stick that stood behind the parlour door. In great terror she brought it to the garden, her hand firmly clutched on the stick, nor could she let it go. Instantly, seeing that the girl was a sensitive, I made a few upward passes over the rod and soon released her hand, which was much cramped, and gave it to my wife. It (the stick) drew her with a very considerable force to nearly the centre of the garden, in a direct line, through currant bushes, over strawberry beds, to a bed of poppies, and there it and she stopped. At that time the phenonema was new to me, and I was as much surprised as any one present, but in answer to my question to my wife why she stood there apparently rooted to the ground, she replied that there was water under the point of that stick, about six feet down in the earth. Some would have said impossible, but we, the gardener and myself, dug down, and found the water as stated. He had given notice to quit, but I advised him to fill the hole up and get a new lease;

he did so, and I left him in possession. The girl had a fearful dread of that hazel rod, nothing could induce her even to touch it. In her superstition she said it was the devil. Thousands besides her think he has something to do with it.

Of course on my return to London such a curious fact to me then, stimulated enquiry, and I instituted a course of experiments, both as regards my wife's clairvoyant power and the action of the hazel rod in the finding of mines, minerals, coal, and springs of water, &c., in fact, by the gift that my wife undoubtedly has, educated myself. I give you without reserve the results.

Experiment 1.—A dry straight stick of hazel was placed in my wife's right hand in a darkened room. She declared that from it proceeded myriads of sparks, and that from each end of it the scintillations emitted were of diverse colours, from the root end red, and from the opposite reddish blue. Deduction—That the hazel rod has two poles, positive and negative.

Experiment 2.—The same rod being held by myself, under the same conditions, she stated that the hazel rod still gave sparks of the same colours, but that they were blended with my own emanations proceeding from myself (which are crimson when in health). Deduction—That the hazel rod can be magnetised even without the will, involuntarily.

Experiment 3.—The same rod, being laid on a table, and a few mesmeric passes made over it, the sensitive stated that its power was much enhanced, and that torrents of sparkles, combined with my red magnetism, covered the whole stick, and to such an extent that the rod was brilliantly luminous. Deduction—That the hazel rod can be impregnated by the human magnetism, and its native power much increased.

Experiment 4.—The same rod being thoughtlessly laid aside, without being demagnetised, it, by its own and my magnetism combined, attracted my wife and compelled her to grasp it, thereby producing catalepsy. This was speedily removed by demagnetising the rod, and making a few upward passes from the feet to the head. Deduction—That the human magnetism is retained by inanimate substances.

Experiment 5.—The same rod being again magnetized by the direction of my wife, and placed in the sun's rays for a few days, and again examined by her, was found to have lost in a very great measure the magnetism imparted to it, though it still retained its own. Deduction—That the sun's rays have the power of restoring substances to their normal condition.

Experiment 6.—A wet or green straight hazel rod was placed in my wife's hand; this produced extreme rigour. Deduction—That the rod when fresh cut *has* inherently a greater force than when dry, but an unpleasant one.

Experiment 7.—The first-named rod having been steeped in water till it was saturated, was found to be equal in force to one freshly cut, causing the same unpleasing sensation. Deduction—That the hazel rod does not loose its power by being dried, and at any time can be restored to its first state.

Experiment 8.—The nuts of the hazel being placed in my wife's hand, produced no results different to other nuts. Deduction.—That the power is in the rod, and not in the fruit. This is analagous to many other plants, as some contain their curative powers in the seeds, others in the roots, others in the bark, &c., some in the whole plant.

Experiment 9.—Rods of willow, alder, aspen, ash, witch elm, saplings of oak, &c., each produced different sensations in the hand of the sensitive, but none equal to the hazel rod. Deduction—That the hazel rod alone should be used for the discovery of mines, minerals, springs, &c.

Experiment 10.—The before-mamed rods, and many other kinds also, both in their green and dry states, on being magnetised, had, by the act of magnetisation, communicated to them a property (by the will, of course) similar but not identical to the hazel rod. Deduction—That the human will can impress a quality to an object that it has not in its normal state, and also until it is demagnetised it will retain it.

Experiment 11.—Rods sawn lengthwise from boards, such as pine, deal, cedar, &c., are polar, but have not their polarity so well marked or distinct as those that have the pith in them. Deduction—A sapling or branch is preferable, having its whole nature in it.*

---

* Allow me here to observe that some woods seem to have the power to retain, and are more congenial to the retention of the effluence proceeding from the hands than others. I might instance acacia and sandal wood as the two best. This has been abundantly proved by numerous experiments since 1860, when *I commenced* to make that most singular psychological instrument, the planchette (see *Spiritual Mag.*, vol. 1, page 228, also planchette in *Once a Week*, Oct. 26, 1866, and my reply to it.

Experiment 12.—A forked hazel rod, on being placed in the sensitive's *hands*, she holding both ends of it, and the point downwards, produced extreme rigidity in the arms and shoulders, with numbness, which continued for days. Deduction—That the sensitive herself, being naturally polar (as all are), and the forked rod polar also, closed the polarity of the sensitive (by the same law as a keeper on a magnet), in fact overpowered her, hence I prefer the straight rod, as it leaves the sensitive the power of comparison.

Experiment 13.—The late Mr. Fradelle, then the Secretary of the Mesmeric Hospital, being present at one of these seances, suggested the hiding of a piece of metal, and the rod being placed in my wife's hand, she could not find it as formerly. Deduction—That the will of the hider magnetises the hidden thing, and so renders it almost impossible for the sensitive to find it.

This explains the repeated failures of those who *can* find metal, their high state of sensitiveness is overborne by those about them either by design, accidentally by too close proximity, or by strong unexpressed doubt.

Will you please to remember that these thirteen experiments were made while my wife was in that state called clairvoyance, induced by mesmerism, and that many other substances were so diagnosed, including medicines, plants, the hidden curative property of them, and their correct application in disease also, and that her power has been repeatedly tested to find minerals, springs, &c., by means of pieces of cane, wire, steel, whalebone, &c., as advised by M. Baritel, but in no case were they successful (the reason will be shown as we proceed). It is my full intention, as I before stated, to render this subject so clear that you can hardly misunderstand me. Possibly I may be tedious; I had rather it were so than not convey my meaning, and be pleased to overlook the frequent use of the *ego* and *meum*, that can scarcely be helped, as the subject is chiefly narrative. At page 102 you will find the method of proceeding to produce the states of psychology or electro biology and mesmerism. The former I should advise you to use if you desire to obtain a sensitive to discover mines, minerals, &c., because, as before stated, so many are *naturally* subject (or can be easily rendered so) to your influence by these simple means. Having asked those who are willing to try if you can biologise them to be seated, place in each person's hand a zinc disc, as described, &c., and having found the one sensitive, place in the right hand (his or her) a straight hazel rod; if it produces rigidity in the hand, or a feeling in the arm, best described as pins and needles, you may be almost sure that you have found the right person. Then proceed, deliberately and cautiously, day by day, to educate your sensitive by such experiments as you may think best, your aim being to discover if they are sensitive to the action of metals; if so, to prove it, throw a piece of money into a dark room, and let your sensitive take the rod in the right hand (the *root* end pointing to the ground—mind this caution) and enter, and, if found, let them retain it— (would you muzzle the ox that treads the corn)—and it would be most advantageous to yourself if the experiment be frequently repeated; or you may walk through the streets with your sensitive with the rod in their hand, when the water is on from the main, and very soon ascertain if they have the power, if so they will follow the course of the water till you wet the end of the stick, which stops its motion; indeed, there is no certain rule. I presume each one must be treated differently to another, according to their temperament and idiosyncrasies. I refrain from giving uncertain instruction, preferring that you study the matter for yourself, which is the only true method of obtaining knowledge of any matter, but it is more than likely that as your sensitive advances they will not need your services, but be able to act without biological induction. But beware of impostors; to detect them mentally *command* them well, say to stand on their head or any other absurd thing, and if they do or attempt to obey your unexpressed *command*, there can be no doubt but that you have the right person. Above all do not deceive yourself nor come to a hasty conclusion, and here I conclude this part of the matter.

About the year 1858 business caused me to form the acquaintance of Dr. Dixon, of Great Ormond-street, to whom I named my wife's faculty. He fully tested it in the cure of diseases, and I give you an extract from his pamphlet, *Hygienic Clairvoyance*.

"25. Intimating my wish to the clairvoyante, Mrs. W., of whom I have already spoken, to investigate, as completely as possible, the natural faculty, possessed by her in so eminent a degree, of *dynamically* perceiving and distinguishing objects, she expressed her willingness. And we arranged for an occasional evening for the purpose. At our first sitting (July 2, 1858) I invited a few friends to be present. Mrs. W. went into an adjoining room while we made preparations. It had been proposed to magnetise her, but she said it was not necessary to be in the sleep to exercise her dynamic faculty; by collecting herself, and *willing*, she could perceive the qualities and magnetoid relations of objects.

"26. Having made our arrangements she was invited to come in. She approached the table; on it were placed, each under a separate piece of paper, and a few inches apart, bismuth, silver, gold, and copper. I had made some transverse passes over each to remove all foreign effluences from them. Putting her hand upon the paper covering the bismuth, she said, 'This feels something like zinc, but I am not sure.' Leaving that, she moved her hand over the paper covering the silver; she said 'Silver is there; it burns because it is so near to this, which must be gold.' Her mistaking the bismuth for zinc, she said, was its being too near the copper. On bringing her hand over the paper concealing the copper, it became cramped and contorted. To relieve this I made transverse passes over the hand and arm, but in vain. 'De-magnetise the copper,' she said. I made transverse passes over the copper, and the cramp of the hand ceased after a few moments. It must be remembered that I had made passes over the copper at the commencement. She said that the metals had all been placed too near each other, that any two metals, she had found, make a battery; the positive with the metals negative to them. She remarked, incidentally, that the sun's rays were the most effective in restoring the proper magnetism to metals; and that, according to her observation, all medicines make batteries with each other; in other words, have positive and negative dynamical relations.

"27. Her faculty not appearing to be sufficiently free from external influence, it was proposed that she should be put into 'the sleep.' For this purpose, on the present occasion, she selected my magnetism, as it was about her since my attempt to free her indirectly from the effluence of the copper. But before magnetising her she wished me to remove my chain, as the effluence from that might affect her; the copper, she said, had made her feel combative.

"28. She passed 'behind the veil,' as I term it, after being magnetised by the eye for something less than a minute. As soon as she intimated, by her usual gesture, that she was in 'the other state,' I proposed that the friends present should place themselves *en rapport* with her, as usual, by touching her hand. 'No,' she said, 'I see and hear you all well enough.' This was unusual, and the reason was not asked, perhaps it lay in the fact of all present being friendly with her, and earnest inquirers into the subject.

"29. She then, at once, reached her hand to a lady, an invalid recovering from a paralytic affection—and said, 'In extreme cases of paralysis a battery like one of these might be worn on the arm, and one of copper and zinc on the thigh, for the battery on the arm will not affect the legs' (her hand here accidentally touched the brass moulding, lined with lead, on the arm of the chair she was in; she shook her hand, blew on it, and said 'Nasty'); there should be a change from time to time; the zinc should sometimes be in contact with the skin, and at other times the copper; the zinc should touch the copper at the edges, but not at the centre. These directions are for a hard, dark person, if fair, reverse the order. In many cases of the loss of the use of the leg and arm, the paralysis is from congestion in the tissues of the brain; in such cases the best battery would be a film of platina on a zinc foundation, with thin paper interposed. Lead and brass make a good battery for some cases also. Mrs. B. (one of the ladies present), should have a thin sheet of brass to her feet, and thin lead to the nape of her neck, and the places to which the metals are applied should be washed at times with camphor water; she would be better in a fortnight.' After a little pause she turned to me and said suddenly, 'Doctor, I have been long enough with metals, you had better awake me, and I will look, after a little time, at anything else.'"

He being pressed with other matters, the seances at his house were discontinued, and I, seeing the value of them in a commercial view, resolved on commencing a course at home, especially as I found her so sensitive as to diagnose the action on her system of a millionth part of a grain of homœopathic medicine —(question, does the infinitely small quantity of the drug act, or is it the will impressed on it, at the time of preparation that does so? I have good reasons for supposing the latter to be the case, they, however,

would be out of place here)—so I procured a homœopathic case and bottles, and put into them about twenty of the metals, each chemically pure (that is without alloy), each of which being placed separately in my wife's hand, produced different results. After a short experience (my will acting, of course) I found that she had the faculty, by the sensations they produced on her, the power of discriminating one from the other with unerring exactitude, and that there was no occasion (as formerly) to put her into that phase of magnetism called clairvoyance. She had the gift at all times, by her own will alone, of finding springs, mines, minerals, &c., on a map of the land being brought to her. This I named to the late Mr. Headland, chemist, of Princes-street, Oxford-street. He doubted it; to convince him my wife sent me for a map of his land, on which he had sunk a very deep Artesian well, and had not found water to supply the houses that he had built (so they were unlet). The map formed sufficient rapport with the land for my wife to *clearly* see it. Her statement was as follows:—
"Tell him that he has sunk the well in the wrong place, and they have not tapped the head of the spring; there is abundance of water; let him sink a fresh well here"—indicating the spot. I took the message to him. His reply was "I will bore for a fresh well if you can give me further particulars." I returned home, and the map was again used, and the following statement in writing was taken by myself to Mr. H. "Outside his land there is a small run of water. This proceeds from an outlet from the hill, on which his houses are built, and now runs to waste."

The strata through which he had bored were described with precision. He admitted it was all true as stated, and did bore for a fresh well, found the water, which is now being used. His shopman then, now a chemist in business for himself in Regent-street, will confirm this statement in every particular. Mr. H. obtained the water by my aid; I received nothing for my trouble, *experientia docet*. However, the matter soon got bruited, and many applications were made, and mines discovered where none were supposed to be—copper, iron, coal, lead, &c.—by the above means, being used. These I may not refer to, having been paid for the same, and it would be a breach of confidence to name the mines discovered by my wife. Do you think that she alone has this faculty? My experience warrants the conviction that there are multitudes, all over the world, of all grades, rich and poor, civilised and barbarous, in whom this power lays latent waiting to be used. Perhaps this small work may stimulate enquiry; for my part I shall be willing to satisfy any reasonable doubts. For the proof of the existence of this power in a far higher degree than I have named, read *Natures Secrets*, by Mr. William Denton, date 1833, Houlston and Wright, publishers. Mr. D. refers in his work to the applicability of this faculty for the finding of metals, &c., and thinks that it will be universally used. As far as I know he has not applied his knowledge practically. It may here be as well to state that the oil wells of Pensylvania were found by one phase of this most precious gift, which, however, is not unattended with danger, for each metal salivates the sensitive, and if an antidote be not at hand most disastrous effects will ensue, and for very fear of the results the sensitive will naturally refuse to continue these researches, and, if the will remained, the power to use it would be destroyed, because the salivation would remain. To obviate this difficulty and annoyance, I think it advisable to say that if your sensitive, who has the power to use the hazel rod only, becomes unable to release his hand from the rod (an occurrence which frequently happens), all that is to be done is to insert into the hand that grasps the rod a small piece of zinc or iron, and if any rigidity still remains make a few upward mesmeric passes, as before described, from the tips of the fingers to the shoulders, and off. This never fails to restore the arm to its normal state; but if your sensitive has the higher, but not more useful, power to dispense with the rod, a very different course must be pursued; as, for instance, if the sensitive has been investigating land (either by the map, or personal visit) which contains gold in excess of other metal, then the antidote to gold must be placed in the hand or other part of the body, at the wish of the sensitive, to relieve the salivation, and instinct will instruct the sensitive far better than you yourself can do (see extract from Dr. Dixon's pamphlet). As a guide, but by no means a certain one, I may remark that gold produces on the sensitive a tingling sensation throughout the whole system, commencing at the spine. The antidote for it is a piece of roll sulphur placed in the hand, or at the base of the neck, for a few minutes. Platina, the same sensation attended with numbness in the spine and extremities; antidote as before, some-

ADDENDA. 125

times cold water. Palladium, nearly the same antidote, ditto. Silver, a cold numbness throughout the region of the heart, and a sensation of heavy weight in the hands and feet; antidote, soda, as before. Lead, without great care in the removal would settle permanently in the system, and would produce a bad salivation, as from Mercury, but more dangerous on account of its heavy nature and non-liability to be ejected from the system; antidote, sulphur and podophyllin taken internally. Mercury, its effects are well known; antidote, great warmth and small doses of milk of sulphur internally until the salivation be removed. Antimony, a most deadly sense of vomiting and utter prostration; antidote, an oyster chewed and ejected, afterwards a few eaten uncooked, let them be natives if possible. Copper, a burning sensation in the throat and tonsils particularly, and also throughout the whole system with great want of power to open the hands; antidote, take internally four or five grains sulphur until relieved. Arsenic, a hot burning sensation in the eyes, throat, and chest, enlargement of the tonsils, in fact, a most deadly feeling throughout the whole system; antidote, mercurius taken internally in small doses until relieved, then sulphur. Tin, a cold icy feeling throughout the whole system, with numbness of the feet; antidote, chloride of sodium (common salt) placed in the hands. Nickel, causes an overflow of blood to the brain, with paralysis of the spinal column and epilepsy; antidote, antimonial wine taken internally in small doses until relieved, in its absence take opium, with natural sleep. Bismuth, a sensation of fulness of blood and congestion of the arteries;

antidote, metallic tin placed in the hands. Graphite, a slight salivation and sense of numbness all over the body; antidote, magnesia, either internally or placed in one or both hands. Cobalt, a disposition for hemorrhage; antidote, a few oysters eaten uncooked, and bathing the hands and face in cold water. Manganese, produces a violent shaking precisely similar to St. Vitus's dance; antidote, chalk held in either or both hands. Iron, produces a sense of tremendous weight all over the body, with disposition to vomit; antidote, a small piece of platina held in either or both hands, or applied to the nape of the neck, or pit of the stomach for a few minutes at a time until relieved. With these few metals I close the list, well aware that there are many others whose properties I have not investigated, as they are comparatively scarce, though I think they would well repay the trouble. Without doubt you will clearly see the danger to the sensitive if the antidotes be not used at the *time* of the experiment being made, as delay aggravates the evil symptoms. The above remarks apply equally to those who have the power to use the hazel rod, or to those who have the clairvoyant power of discovering mines, minerals, &c.; and here let me caution you when you have found the sensitive not to use the gift more than twice monthly, or the power will be soon destroyed. A few words as to its application, and my task is finished. It is evident by the testimony given that there exists a power possessed by some (thousands, in reality) to find springs, mines, and minerals by means of the hazel rod, and I think that I have shown that some have also the power to do so with much more certainty by clairvoyance, or a

ADDENDA.

waking state in which sensitives have the power, by the exercise of their own will, to place themselves *en rapport* with distant objects, and the metals being almost all poisonous, and to all violently active, of necessity attacks *their* sensitiveness in a great degree; self-introvision and practice enables them to see their own state and describe it. This is my experience of the matter, and (in my opinion) a solution of the apparent mystery. What is more easy than to usefully apply it? Let us suppose three cases. A shaft has been sunk and the mineral not found, and of course the capital wasted. With the utmost facility I declare it can be known, firstly, if there be any metal or mineral near, or in sufficient quantity to pay for the getting; secondly, if its depth be such that it would cost more to get than it would be worth, with the capital in hand; or eventually, thirdly, it can be known whether it would be advisable to sink a shaft in any given place on account of the proximity of springs which might overflow; and lastly, in mines already worked the true position, place, locality, quantity, and quality of ores and minerals can be given. Surely this is worth attention, and the *modus operandi* a searching study, for if my statements be true, illimitable wealth is of easy acquirement.* Were I commencing the study of the subject, I would procure a few biological discs, as before described, a few hazel rods, and a homœopathic case, containing about two dozen corked (not stoppered) bottles, with a small quantity of chemically pure metals in eighteen of them, the rest empty for the antidotes.

---

* Indeed, at this present time, to my certain knowledge, I know of an estate of 300 acres in extent, enormously rich in silver, lead, gold, and Barytes, and which requires but small capital to realize *very* large sums of money; it can also be had on easy terms, or a portion of it. The metal is actually on the surface, native, and can be seen with the naked eye.

These I should be willing to supply on application. Indeed, my researches have not been confined to these few metals only, but to many other substances, and by the art which I have endeavoured to teach you, have sought the world over, and affirm that (judging from the past) the pyramid in the Exhibition of 1862, representing the gold found in Australia, is a mere molehill compared with what one day *will* be found when the science that I have brought before your notice will be the usual method (for *I* have not exhausted the subject, merely called your attention to it) of discovering the minerals, &c., and if gold be wealth (which I doubt) it is in almost illimitable quantities in the lands adjacent to Ashantee, in Siam also, in Assam and Burmah prodigious quantities of gold, rubies of price. Silver (but not much), lead, copper, manganese, graphite, gold, copper, kaolin, potter's clay, masses of minerals and coal also in Australia. Plenty of it too in Batavia, China, Japan, and of good quality, illimitable wealth spread all over the earth, requiring but trivial labour to obtain it. But why *should* we seek wealth in other lands, when our own islands teem with it, and at home to our very hands, why is so little obtained of it, and at such great expense. Simply because they blunder in the getting of it, and the lodes are not worked out to their terminations in many cases. Why does the water so frequently inundate the mines, causing such enormous outlay to keep them clear? Simply because our present knowledge in most cases does not teach us how to evade the springs. Why not bore for them first, and bring them to the surface, before commencing to sink a shaft for the mineral. That such can be done with almost unerring certainty is my object in indicting these few pages, which are but preliminary (to the subject treated), being fully investigated, such is my conviction.

www.ingramcontent.com/pod-product-compliance
Lightning Source LLC
Chambersburg PA
CBHW071351080526
44587CB00017B/3053